Information, Knowledge, Text

Julian Warner

The Scarecrow Press, Inc.
Lanham, Maryland, and London
2001

SCARECROW PRESS, INC.

Published in the United States of America
by Scarecrow Press, Inc.
4720 Boston Way, Lanham, Maryland 20706
www.scarecrowpress.com

4 Pleydell Gardens, Folkestone
Kent CT20 2DN, England

British Library Cataloguing in Publication Information Available

Library of Congress Cataloging-in-Publication Data

Warner, Julian, 1955–
   Information, knowledge, text / Julian Warner.
      p. cm. – (A Scarecrow book)
   Includes index.
   ISBN 0-8108-3989-X (alk. paper)
      1. Written communication. I. Title. II. Series.

   P211 . W336 2001
   302.2'244—dc21

                                                            00-067055

⊖™ The paper used in this publication meets the minimum requirements of
American National Standard for Information Sciences—Permanence of
Paper for Printed Library Materials, ANSI/NISO Z39.48-1992.
Manufactured in the United States of America.

Contents

Figures

Acknowledgments

I would like to thank Aslib, the Association for Information Management, for permission to adapt articles first published by them.

Chapter 1 is a republication, with slight editorial alterations, of: Julian Warner. "Studying writing." *Journal of Documentation* 53 (2), 1997, 226-237.

Chapter 6 includes: Julian Warner. Review of Samuel Johnson. *A dictionary of the English language on CD-ROM.* 1st (1755) and 4th (1773) editions, edited by A. McDermott. Cambridge: Cambridge University Press, 1996. *Journal of Documentation.* 53 (5), 1997, 558-561; and Julian Warner. Review of Clifford A. Lynch. "Accessibility and integrity of networked information collections." *Journal of Documentation* 55 (1), 1995, 68-72.

Chapter 7 is an edited and shortened version of: Julian Warner. "Is there an origin to graphic communication." *Managing Information* 1 (2), 1994, pp. 32-34.

I would like to thank John Wiley and Sons, Inc. for permission to reprint an article and reviews.

Chapter 4 is a republication, with slight editing, of Julian Warner. "Writing and literary work in copyright: A binational and historical analysis." *Journal of the American Society for Information Science* 44 (6), 1993, 307-321. © John Wiley and Sons, Inc. 1993.

Chapter 6 includes: Julian Warner. Review of Yorick A. Wilks, Brian M. Slator, and Louise M. Guthrie. "Electric words: Dictionaries, computers, and meanings." *Journal of the American Society for Information Science* 47 (10), 1996, 791-792. © John Wiley and Sons, Inc. 1996; Julian Warner. Review of Brian Kahin and Charles Nesson editors. "Borders in cyberspace: Information policy and the global information infrastructure." *Journal of the American Society for Information Science* 49 (11), 1998, 387-388. © John Wiley and Sons, Inc. 1998; and Julian Warner. Review of Paul Levinson. "The soft edge: A natural history and future of the Information Revolution." *Journal of the American Society for Information Science* 49 (11), 1998, 1041. © John Wiley and Sons, Inc. 1998.

I would also like to acknowledge the American Society for Information Science:

An earlier version of chapter 2 was given as an oral presentation to the Annual Conference of the American Society for Information Science, Arlington, Virginia, October 1994.

An earlier version of chapter 3 was also given as an oral presentation to the Annual Conference of the American Society for Information Science, Chicago, October 1995.

I would also like to acknowledge Routledge:

Parts of chapter 4 appeared in Julian Warner. *From Writing to Computers*. London: Routledge, 1994.

An earlier version of this chapter was also given to the seminar, Informatics and Semiotics held at Schloss Dagstuhl, International Conference and Research Center for Computer Science in February 1996 (Seminar no. 9608, Report no. 135).

Preface

This work emerges from a concern with the challenge posed by D. F. McKenzie in the 1985 Panizzi lectures, subsequently published as *Bibliography and the Sociology of Texts*:

> Panizzi . . . would not . . . have simply accepted computing as just another technological aid, one more efficient than others for doing certain jobs. He would have asked: on what unifying, intellectual principle, does it relate to books?

> (McKenzie 1986: 42)

McKenzie's proposal for a sociology of texts received a mixed reception, partly sympathetic, but also critical, although the work has been increasingly cited, particularly in the humanities. Its central challenge was addressed in a previous monographic publication by the present author, *From Writing to Computers* (Warner 1994), itself subject to a wider variation in reception.

At the level of practical understanding, computing and other modern information technologies have been partly further assimilated to historical and still continuing technological forms since 1985 and 1994. Naturalization has occurred through diffusion and use. Similarly, the legal distinctions between computer-held and paper data, which troubled McKenzie, have been reduced. At the theoretical and epistemological level, understanding still needs deliberately to be developed. The focus must be on social, not individual, epistemology, on collective, not personal, ways of knowing. Naturalization of technologies can even work against recognizing and addressing such issues by reducing their strangeness.

This collection continues to develop the themes of *From Writing to Computers*, but through a series of studies rather than a fully developed further thesis. For instance, at the epistemological level, exactness is identified as a crucial factor linking, and differentiating, primary orality from literacy as communication by written language, and as crucial to the development and possibilities of computation. Information technologies are fully recognized as a human construction. The thesis of *From Writing to Computers* is rendered more robust and the project anticipated in "An information view of history" (Warner 1999) can be seen to emerge.

The opening chapter, "Studying Writing," establishes the intellectual context for subsequent chapters. "Shannon, Weaver, and the Minotaur: Redundancy in Language and Information Systems" then addresses the past and present of writing and signal transmission and issues connected with information theory and its influence on the development of information science. "Not the Exact Words . . . : Writing, Computing, and Exactness" identifies exactness as a crucial feature not fully anticipated in primary orality, enabled and encouraged by writing, with computing both enhancing the possibilities for exactness and simultaneously revealing the fluidity and inconsistency of human semiotic constructions.

"Toward an Integrated Account of Formal Logic and Automata Theory: Iconic and Notational Models" applies to different forms of representation in formal logic and automata studies, which, it is argued, have inhibited the development of an integrated understanding. "Writing and Literary Work in Copyright: A Binational and Historical Analysis" then conducts a close empirical study of the history of the interpretation of writing and of a work in which intellectual property can inhere in United States and United Kingdom copyright, with the historical rigor of the study intended as a counterbalance to the broader theoretical excursions, and inevitably revealing the untidy complexity of the subject addressed. The 1870s and 1880s also emerge as a crucial period for the diffusion of modern information technologies. "Is There an Origin to Graphic Communication?" briefly reviews the past of graphic communication. The concluding chapter "Reviews" continues to explore themes established. The chronological order of the reviews, after the first review of Johnson's *A Dictionary of the English*

Language on CD-ROM, reveals the emergence of a Marxian view of technology as a human construction, although not its yet unexplored analogies and contrasts with the social construction of technology movement.

All the chapters have previously undergone editorial and, in many cases, full peer review as either journal articles or conference presentations. The original papers have been carefully edited for republication to avoid repetition and increase coherence, including indicating connections between chapters. Where papers were originally prepared for spoken delivery, and have not previously been made public in written form, a sufficient degree of exactness has been imposed for written publication.

Journal articles and conference presentations were originally directed primarily, although not exclusively, to the information science community. Here the intention is to re-address that community in more coherent form, reach other disciplinary, and possibly wider public, fora through monographic publication, and lend permanence to previously only spoken publications.

The perspective adopted by the work stresses continuity rather than radical disjunctions in information technologies and is informed by the implications of Walter Benjamin's remark that, "within the phenomenon [of the possibilities of replication of art objects] which we are here examining from the perspective of world history, print is merely a special, though particularly important, case" (Benjamin 1936: 219). Although the scope for willed or imposed change might be limited, information technologies can be used to good or ill. The fuller the understanding of information developments, the more deliberately and, possibly, productively they can be directed or, at least, accommodated. In this context, man is restored as artificer of elaborate systems of thought and of information technologies and as architect of his own history.

Chapter 1

Studying Writing

Introduction

These two works by Roy Harris, *The Origin of Writing* (Harris 1986) and *Signs of Writing* (Harris 1995), represent a sophisticated, although difficult, treatment of the nature of writing, including the recognition of nonverbal forms of writing and the relation of verbal forms of writing to speech. A citation analysis and informed reading indicates that their importation into information science literature has been limited, with some, rather isolated, exceptions (see chapters 2 and 3; Warner 1994). Yet there is the possibility of some substantial mutual connections.

Information science itself has been characterized as a partly unreflexive response to developments in computer and telecommunications technology in the late 1940s. As part of a reaction against this lack of reflexivity, the status of programming as a non-verbal form of writing has recently received some attention (see chapter 5; Warner 1994). Conversely, discussions of writing could have been more fully informed by themes developed within the information science literature: for instance, the conversation model of scholarly communication (Wilson 1983) can assist an understanding of commonalities and contrasts between speech and writing; and the intentions reconstructed in *The Origin of Writing* (Harris 1986) for the devisors of alphabetic writing bear similarities to the conditions established for the economic transmission of signals in *The Mathematical Theory of Communication* (Shannon and Weaver 1949) (see chapter 2).

The difficulty of the Harris's works lies partly in their terminology and theoretical context, which draws upon semiology and Saussurean linguistics. From this perspective, *Signs of Writing* is more difficult than the earlier and both more coherently and colloquially written *The Origin of Writing*. The historical scope of both works might also be relatively unfamiliar to information science. However, a more fundamental difficulty would seem to be rooted in the nature of Western literacy.

Western literacy tends to involve the "integration in consciousness of speech with writing" (Harris 1986: 51). On a discursive, scholarly level, this is partly embodied in the classic Aristotelian view of writing as a secondary representation of speech. Less formally, but possibly more powerfully, acquisition of written language tends to stress its connection with spoken sounds. Non-verbal forms of writing, for instance logical notations or computer programming languages, may be acquired at less crucially formative stages of education, although they may still be given verbal and oral correlates for the purposes of written and spoken discussion. Disentangling writing from speech may therefore involve a struggle with received consciousness.

Some other inheritances from Aristotelian methods of thought and ideas in common discourse may also account for their difficulty. The notion of the purity of categories, associated with the Aristotelian insistence on classification and subsequently widely adopted (Hasan 1987: 116-117), can obstruct understanding. It can be detected in the search for a set of characteristics that will consistently differentiate speech from writing and in the rigidity of some of Harris's own categorizations. It would seem to require an oral fluidity to admit that marginal cases may defy categorization—one thinks, for instance, of George Bush inviting viewers to: "Read my lips–no new taxes." Less exclusively associated with Aristotle, yet present in the view of writing as a secondary representation of speech, is the notion of semiotic dependence, that one sign system is derivative from another, which is found also in other contexts, for instance in understandings of African drum language (Finnegan 1970).

Yet the difficulty of the works and the complexity of the issues addressed is matched by their significance. Let us, then, critically summarize and evaluate them, beginning with the earlier *The Origin of Writing* and moving on to *Signs of Writing*, while also considering their broader intellectual context.

The Origin of Writing

Harris's first chapter, "From folklore to technology," considers fictional accounts of the origin of writing, from Kipling's *Just So* stories to Edgar Rice Burroughs's *Tarzan*, and detects assumptions common in the Western tradition in these narratives: for instance, that speech is historically prior to writing and that writing originated as a communicative substitute for speech. Less noticed is a preoccupation with origins, although the existence of an origin to graphic communication has been questioned in other contexts (see chapter 7). A crucial point made is that obscurity about the origin of writing is created by not regarding it as problematic at all, as a transparent representation of objects in the case of hieroglyphics or of spoken sounds with the alphabet. Although writing may function as a communicative substitute for speech, technically it is a development from drawing or, more broadly, from graphic art. When contrasted with speech, the crucial communicative advantages of writing are seen to lie in its independence of a specific point in space and time, with the autonomous text substituting for a live speaker. More could have been made of the distinction between space and time and between other dimensions of communicative significance: For instance, a significant, but unnoticed, contrast between the message is carried by Bellerophon in the *Iliad*, for secret transmission over space (Warner 1994: 47-50), and the adoption of writing for the communal preservation of the *Koran* over time (Harris 1986: 15-22). Even Hermes the messenger can be contrasted with the recordkeeping and time-related functions associated with the Egyptian (and historically earlier) Thoth (Griffith 1911). The rhetorical strategy here and elsewhere in *The Origin of Writing* would seem to be to engender a *Verfremdungs-Effekt*, to make writing and its relation to speech unfamiliar and to disturb received notions found within Western literacy.

The second chapter is concerned with "The tyranny of the alphabet." By this is understood the alphabetical teleology, the regarding of the alphabet as the "last and most important stage of writing" (Diringer 1968, Volume 1: 13), which has influenced previous discussions of writing in the Western tradition. Established classifications of forms of writing, for instance, as logographic, pictographic, or ideographic, are shown to derive, directly or indirectly, from an initial, and partly covert, contrast with alphabetic forms (Harris 1986: 37). Even the idea of the syllable as having constituent units is identified as an alphabetic notion which reverses the historical order of the development of the two forms (Harris 1986: 39). A crucial point made is that the view of writing as a representation of speech is effectively scriptist (giving covert priority to writing for the purposes of linguistic analysis) if alphabetic writing is taken as a perfect, or near-perfect, representation of speech. The idea of an alphabetic tyranny might seem easier to distance, once identified, than the integration in speech and writing in consciousness, yet there are traces of both in Harris's own work. *The Origin of Writing* is, despite its title, primarily concerned with the development of the alphabet from other forms of writing and gives little attention to non-verbal forms of writing (*Signs of Writing* contrasts in this respect). The uncritical treatment of the word as a concept could be said to betray some influence from written language, particularly from those forms that have marked word boundaries.

Some unnoticed assumptions seem also to be inherited from scholarly linguistic discussions. For instance, it is convincingly suggested that "the notion of an ideal alphabet holding up a mirror to phonetic reality is based on the assumption that in phonetic reality we find an antecedently given set of individual sounds" (Harris 1986: 38). Yet the further possibility, strongly suggested by a reading of narratives surviving from primary orality and by empirical observations of oral societies, that the isolation and abstraction of phonetic reality from the existential context of oral discourse, which is found in influential components of linguistics (Volosinov 1929), is itself a literate move, connected with influence of decontextualized written language, is only fleetingly remarked. The possibility of diachronic change in phonetic reality, once isolated as an object of study, in such features as stability over time and systematicity, with written language acting as an influence to reduce variety, is also not considered. Yet Samuel Johnson referred to non-literate speakers who "catch sounds imperfectly . . . (and) utter them negligently" (Johnson 1755a: 4). Accounts of the transcription of previously purely oral American Indian languages can also be read to reveal their lack of systematicity (Boas 1911: 12-20).

The limited attention given to the social dimensions of oral and written communication, not differentiating, for instance, between time and space dimensions and the extent of interaction between participants in communication, could also be connected to the abstraction of utterance from its social context for linguistic study.

The third chapter, "The evolutionary fallacy," is concerned with accounts of the development of full, or alphabetic, writing from preexisting forms of writing. Again, a dual relation to the tyranny of the alphabet can be detected: existing accounts are correctly indicted of an alphabetical teleology, of seeing historically preceding written forms as imperfect products of a striving toward the alphabet, yet Harris's focus of attention is upon the emergence of alphabetic forms (and there continues to be an unnoticed assumption that the sounds of utterance exist ahistorically as isolated objects for study). The distinctions customarily made between types of writing, such as pictography, ideography, and logography, are seen as unhelpful and to complicate an explanation of the transition to full writing. Some subtle and significant points are made. Iconic characters, where a character is said to recall a notion associated with the object visually represented, betray the influence of the double symbolism association with discussions of the relation of alphabetic writing to speech. The rebus, where an image of an object is said to be interpreted by its associated pronunciation, is based on random identities of form and does offer a systematic basis for a transition to a phonographic script. A recurrent theme, which emerges without being fully developed, is that the context and history of production of signs can be highly significant to their interpretation. In this context, it should be recalled that Twain's parody of nineteenth-century deciphering of ancient scripts rests on the decontextualized form in which the samples of scripts are encountered by the actors of the narrative (Twain 1875; Warner 1994: 96). A further point could be derived from critiques of the deciphering of ancient scripts: the view of language as a series of self-identical forms may be an essential methodological assumption in deciphering that language but need not be regarded as a description of it (Volosinov 1929); similarly, a connection to the sounds of utterance may be a helpful (possibly not essential) assumption in establishing equivalences between written signs but should not be taken as an account of the synchronic interpretation of those signs. Substitutional tables could themselves be regarded as an indication of the possibility of obtaining equivalences between written signs without recourse to speech. Overarching themes that can be read from the accounts of forms of writing would be: that a semiotic impulse toward significant order underlies the variety of graphic and oral communication; and that there may not be an origin to writing, in that it is always possible to find antecedent forms of coded graphic communication (see chapter 7; Diringer 1968: Volume 1-4).

The fourth chapter, "Writing as representation," is both complex and crucial. It gives a critique of received notions of the relation between writing and speech and then a positive reconstruction of the motivations of the devisors of alphabetic writing. The classic Aristotelian doctrine of written language as a secondary representation of speech is criticized: it is insufficiently clear on what is represented and rests on the untenable assumption that speech is a series of discrete sounds. Attempts to recover the doctrine by clarifying what is represented, for instance, by asserting an iconic relation between the position of the articulatory organs and the shape of the corresponding letter or by replacing the notion of representation by correlation, are found to present comparable difficulties to those avoided. A further point made, which could have been more fully developed, is that we speak and write with the whole body and that speech is, in this sense, no less visible than writing. Some additional points that might have added conviction to the argument could have been made. For instance, it is possible to distinguish the process of transcription from pronunciation. It can then be recognized that pronunciation is more readily acquired in modern individual educational development and may have longer historical antecedents than verbatim transcription. In the process of pronunciation, writing is also functioning partly as a primary semiotic system. Additionally, a stronger distinction between those factors involved in the origin of alphabetic writing and in its sustainment, extending to recognition that acceptance of the alphabetic principle may affect the production of speech as a human activity, would also have been helpful.

Once the notion of writing as representation is disposed of, the issues of the relation of the alphabet to speech and of what motivated its devisors are addressed. Traces of a preoccupation with origins and of an alphabetic tyranny can be detected, but the cultural significance of the alphabet should simultaneously be acknowledged. The motivations of the inventors of alphabetic writing are reconstructed by considering the internal semiology of the alphabet. Letters of the alphabet are not hierarchically or relationally ordered but are independent and equipollent characters intended to be used in free sequential combination. It is then argued that the devisors of alphabetic writing were concerned with writing as writing and were not influenced by the alphabetic principle as it has been subsequently understood of one letter to one sound, but that alphabetic writing still had some connection with speech. There are some unnoticed similarities with the themes and terminology of information theory and specifically of *The Mathematical Theory of Communication* and the possibility of deeper resemblances has been explored elsewhere (see chapter 2). Again, a stronger distinction between conditions for origin and for sustainment would have added conviction to the argument. Some unnoticed assumptions are of the preexistence of letters to a script, of a script to its use, and that the distinction of the number of letters in a script is unproblematic. Yet the reconstruction of the intentions of the devisors of alphabetic writing from the internal semiology of the alphabet is rich and convincing and deserves further amplification and exploration.

The fifth chapter, "The great invention," is no longer primarily focused upon the alphabet but discusses the development of forms of writing, and then the alphabet, from historically prior types of graphic signification. The reluctance of scholars to acknowledge writing as an invention is noticed and could have been more strongly linked to a similar reluctance by linguists to acknowledge spoken language as a human construction. The concern is no longer directly with the internal semiology of the alphabet but with the emergence of writing from emblematic forms. The distinction between writing and pictures is discussed and found to be problematic and historically variable; the assumption of the natural priority of iconic images is also found to be untenable. The emergence of writing from emblems and tokens is traced to the increasing demands on these systems and the disruption of graphic isomorphism, of a resemblance between a sign and its object, by their elaboration. A final position is formulated: that graphic signs have no other semiological constraints in their use for human communication other than those that derive causally from their nature as graphic marks. From this perspective, verbal forms of writing can be seen as those that draw on models in oral discourse for the purposes of graphic communication (Harris 1986: 122-151).

In some respects, this chapter is less satisfying, less convincing, and more speculative than previous chapters. Visual signs prior to the development of writing other than emblems and tokens, for instance, natural objects and utilitarian artifacts taken as signs (see chapter 7), are neglected. The significance of the distinction between time and space dimensions in communication could have been more fully explored. A paleographer might also insist that written signs need only be visually recoverable, often with the assistance of contextual information, not visually identifiable.

Signs of Writing

Signs of Writing contrasts in a number of respects with *The Origin of Writing*. It is more deliberately and explicitly theoretical, without a comparably specific empirical focus. The theoretical distinctions made were not fully developed in *The Origin of Writing*, although they may have partially and implicitly informed the earlier work. The more technical vocabulary and less colloquial style suggest a different genesis, perhaps from a set of lectures, and a contrasting, more narrowly academic, intended audience. There can also be a higher level of presumed contextual knowledge in the reader: for instance, an understanding of the Aristotelian view of writing as a secondary symbolism is assumed. Despite these contrasts, there are some continuities in methodological difficulties from *The Origin of Writing*. There can be a similar insistence on purity of categories, for instance in the distinctions made between the "integrational" approach adopted and Saussurean semiology and in some of the contrasts made between signatures and oral commitments, and these can tend to rigidify and detract from arguments that might otherwise be more fully convincing. Empirical testing of the theoretical framework developed is advanced as the next stage. The work lends itself to an evaluative critique rather than an exhaustive summary.

The integrational approach that explicitly informs *Signs of Writing* is initially developed by a series of contrasts with Saussurean semiology. It is not telementational, an approach that would consider communication as the transfer of thoughts from one individual's mind to another's, does not isolate the communicative act from its context, and does not insist on an identity between thoughts or signs transmitted and received. Rather it views communication as the contextualized integration of human activities by means of signs. An understanding of the communicative context can be liberally informed, without methodological restrictions on the relevance of evidence, and different analyses of sign appropriate to particular contexts are encouraged (Harris 1995: 1-24).

From an integrational perspective, reading and writing are viewed as biomechanically independent: it is physically possible to read or write without being capable of the other activity. However, as constituents of the process of communications, they are linked by a relation of reciprocal presupposition: writing assumes the possibility of reading and reading the existence of writing. Signs are treated as the products of reading and writing and not as entities that preexist those activities. Some attention could have been given to non-linguistic forms of reading, for instance, in the interpretation of natural signs, which might also have indicated that reading, in this broader sense, can pre-exist writing and the transcription of utterance (see chapter 7). In the terms of *Signs of Writing*, reading could be regarded as the opening possibility for the development of writing. Refreshingly, psychologists' view of writing and reading is indicted for its ethnocentricity and for receiving the sign as a given, rather than as something demanding explanation (Harris 1995: 14-20).

Three aspects to a theory of writing are distinguished: a theory of written communication, a theory of the written sign, and a theory of writing systems. Let us, then, consider the scope and value of each of these three aspects in turn (Harris 1995: 27-28).

A theory of written communication is concerned with the "general requirements for the production and interpretation of written texts" (Harris 1995: 28). A version of a theory of written communication is initially developed by transposing Saussure's model of the speech circuit into a writing circuit of communication, but this is found inadequate in some crucial respects. First, writing, in contrast to speech, generally requires the use of tools for its production. The depth of this particular contrast (which seems to imply the apparent naturalness of speech) could be reduced by acknowledging that man can be regarded as biologically adapted rather than biologically designed for speech (Volosinov 1929). Second, the limited social diffusion of competence in writing as contrasted with speech means that the act of writing can have significance independent of its content; and historical and fictional examples are given to illustrate this. From an integrational perspective, political, social, or religious circumstances cannot be excluded from consideration without decontextualizing the process of written communication and no a priori constraints are set on what is admissible as evidence. Nor is communication conceived in terms of shared identities between sender and receiver (Harris 1995: 28-30, 33-37). The integrational approach outlined promises to offer a fuller, more open-ended, and less methodologically constrained perspective on writing than could be obtained from the Saussurean model initially formulated.

A theory of the written sign is concerned with the "form and meaning of the units of writing" (Harris 1995: 27). The commonalities and contrasts Saussure makes between spoken and written signs are recounted: both are bipartite units, and signifier and signified would normally be distinguished (Warner 1994), but the written sign is visual, not aural, and is only an indirect representation of thought through the spoken sign directly represented (Harris 1995: 31). More broadly, surrogational and structural perspectives on the sign are distinguished. From a surrogational perspective, signs are conceived as something standing for something else. In contrast, a structural perspective is concerned with mutual differentiations between signs (Harris 1995: 50-52). The sharp boundary made between these models could be questioned and the possibility of understandings of the sign being informed by both surrogational and structural models could have been explored. The structural model has been considered particularly appropriate to an understanding of writing: characters, for instance, can be considered as units identifiable by their mutual differences (Harris 1995: 52). An integrational approach, by contrast, treats the sign as depending on the context in which it is produced and views communication as the dynamic process in which signs are created (Harris 1995: 52-55). Again, such an approach has the value of contextualizing written communication and could be informed by those elements of the surrogational and structural perspectives that are considered appropriate to the particular contexts studied.

A theory of writing systems is concerned with the "semiological differences between one script and another" (Harris 1995: 27), and, further, with the semiological differentiae that permit a typology of different kinds of writing to be constructed. Classically, distinctions have been made between phonetic and non-phonetic writing, for example, in Saussure's contrast of ideographic with non-phonetic forms. One deficiency of this approach to categorization is its neglect of non-glottic forms of writing, that is, forms of writing only remotely related to spoken language (which would include computer-programming languages). A further, and possibly deeper, misleading assumption is that the structure of a writing system can be established by the correlation between its graphic units and some non-written medium. An integrational approach, by contrast, focuses on the similarities and differences with which various kinds of writing use the graphic space available. For instance, *boustrophedon* (the way the ox-drawn plough moves) would be distinguished from *non-boustrophedon* writing even if an identical or highly similar set of characters is used (Harris 1995: 56-64). The discussion implies, although it does not explicitly state, that distinctions made between systems of writing may depend on the level of analysis required. The value of an integrational approach would seem to lie in its concentration upon what is common to many forms of writing, their deployment of graphic space, regardless of the interpretation— whether, for instance, oral or musical—that may be assigned to those forms of writing.

The value of these distinctions (and other components of a theory of writing could, and are, proposed) would seem to lie partly in the clarity of focus of attention enabled. Topics of interest may still transgress boundaries between components. Further valuable methodological distinctions are made within the components distinguished. For instance, within the theory of writing systems, a notation is distinguished from the script or scripts in which it is used. The alphabet as a notation can then be distinguished from its use in the script of written English or from the use of a subset in Roman numerical notation. The structuring that belongs to the notation can then be distinguished from the structuring that belongs to the scripts: in this instance, alphabetical order could be differentiated from the ordering imposed by scripts in either written English or Roman notation for number (Harris 1995: 102-105). Analogies could be found in areas of study more familiar to information science, for instance, in the distinction between an alphabet of symbols and the rules for their combination found in automata theory and logical symbolism. Potential contributions from information science to a theory of writing would seem likely to fall under a theory of written communication or a theory of writing systems rather than a theory of the written sign. Under the theory of written communication, the conversation model of scholarly communication can provide an unnoticed analogue to the time related and intra-individual communication embodied in a private written diary: with some scholarly work, the interested community may be identical with the individual and publication can be regarded as a public conversation between a single individual at different points in time (Wilson 1983). Within a theory of writing systems, information science could contribute to an enhanced understanding of the structure of alphabetic written language, particularly with regard to the value of redundancy in communication (see chapter 2).

Some methodological difficulties are continuous with *The Origin of Writing*. Reading and writing are biomechanically distinguished but the possibility of different effects of reading and writing on patterns of thought is not indicated, although the social implications of literacy are not its primary concern. The contrast made in Bacon's apothegm, "reading maketh a full man . . . writing an exact man" (Bacon 1597: 153), might have been instructive here, although Bacon's concern is with the literate individual not with a social transition from pre-literacy to literacy in the sense of communication by written language (see chapter 3). The reading of non-written signs is again not explored. Pronunciation in the sense of reading from written to oral signs is not sufficiently distinguished from the transcription of oral discourse to written signs. Yet *Signs of Writing* does provide a theoretical context for systematic study of some of these distinctions.

Traces of an influence from an insistence on purity of categories can also be detected. For instance, it is argued that the structuralist model in which signs derive their value from their mutual contrast with a system necessarily implies a fixed-code model of signification with a determinate inventory of signs (change brings a new system into existence). In contrast, an integrational model is an open-code model that does not insist upon a system with a determinate number of members (Harris 1995: 54-55). More flexibly, even from a structuralist perspective, the concept of a system of signs could be regarded as a valuable regulatory idea rather than a real existent, and, on this understanding, could be adapted to an integrational approach. Similarly, it is asserted that there is no corresponding act in spoken language to the written signature and the significance of vows in oral societies is neglected. The value of a signature is said to be that it cannot prevaricate or renege (Harris 1995: 80-84). A similar value was attached to written political charters in *The Origin of Writing*. Yet a crucial factor common to the effect of written signatures and charters and to vows in oral societies might be the continuing assent of relevant interpretative communities. An appeal to a written signature or charter can be regarded as one argument that might be used in securing that assent. The dichotomies made between signatures and oral commitments could then, more convincingly, be rendered as a series of contrasts. Traces of abstract objectivism could even be found in the stress on the autonomous significance of the signature.

More flexibly, the Aristotelian insistence on final definition is avoided. A consistent distinction is made between terminological and conceptual issues. A crucial point that informs *Signs of Writing* is explicitly made toward the end of the work:

> when a new feature or set of features acquires significance in the formation of the written message–the semiological domain of writing is *eo ipso* extended. That is why any attempt to restrict the scope of semiological analysis by an *a priori* definition of writing must be rejected; for such a restriction fails to come to terms with the open-endedness of the very phenomenon it purports to investigate.

(Harris 1995: 161)

It could also be noted that human semiotic and technological activity can change and, increasingly, is changing boundaries between speech and writing and that this is liable to frustrate attempts at stable definition.

A postscript addresses the position associated with Walter Ong (Ong 1982; 1986) and is subject to an incisive earlier critique by Harris (1989) that writing restructures thought. In this context, the position is seen as a particular instance of a more general proposition that "all new intellectual tools restructure thought." A more satisfying question is then substituted: "how does *this* innovation make possible or foster forms of thought that were previously difficult or impossible?" (Harris 1995: 166). A valuable, although brief, enumeration of the effects that might be expected to be associated with writing on the basis of an integrational analysis is given. The possibility that the series of contrasts made by Bacon might be crucial to an understanding of the effects associated with writing, and with contemporary information technologies, is not noticed. In other contexts, it has been suggested that exactness associated with writing was an essential preliminary to the construction of sophisticated information technologies, including modern computers, and to the development of formal logic, automata theory, and programming languages. In its application, computing can both enable increased exactness, for instance, permitting a more precise discrimination of the number and other characteristics of records in a catalogue, and can also encourage fluidity, with, for example, the rapid diachronic succession of frequently revised public files contrasting with the longer intervals between more clearly discrete editions of printed works (see chapter 3; Warner 1994: 114).

Empirical application of the theoretical framework developed in *Signs of Writing* is advanced as a further stage. Refinement of both empirical and theoretical understanding might be expected from a dialectic between the two. For instance, non- and quasi-glottic forms of writing, such as the matrix of marks on musical rolls and telegraphic codes that have been regarded as antecedents to computer programming languages for the purposes of copyright, have been studied in that context (see chapter 5). An integrational analysis could be applied to these forms of writing; and the question of whether an integrational, ordinary discourses or legal understanding is most informative, and for what purposes, could then be addressed. The question of the semiological unity of forms of writing is opened here but not fully concluded, although the possibility of integrational analysis is demonstrated. Whether there is a shared, even if minimal, set of cultural characteristics associated with writing is a further issue.

Integrational analysis promises to reveal, and has begun to reveal, the diversity of forms and functions associated with writing.

Conclusion

In relation to other literature, both works are well rooted in their relevant scholarly context and their citations have value as routes to further information. There are some significant omissions, not necessarily usually considered within linguistics or information science. V. N. Volosinov's *Marxism and the Philosophy of Language* can be said to have partially anticipated an integrational approach, particularly in its insistence on contextualizing linguistic communication and in regarding spoken language not as self-identical signals but as variable and mutable signs (Volosinov 1929). Giambattista Vico's *The New Science* would also seem to be relevant for its insistence on signification as a condition of social man, historical priority of writing to speech, and alphabetic written language as epistolary communication across space (Vico 1744).

Neither work is easy to digest nor fully comprehended here, and both conflict with culturally, deeply ingrained notions of writing and the relations between writing and speech. Yet the final two challenges offered by *Signs of Writing*, namely, to conduct theoretically informed empirical studies and address the question of what is distinctive about modes of thought enabled by current information technologies, can be addressed within information science. A historical and theoretical awareness can help information science to escape from being an unreflexive response to developments in information technology. As Harris notes, conceptualization of changes tends to lag behind the technical changes that have partially motivated them (Harris 1995: 41), but information science should be able to contribute to closing that distance.

Chapter 2

Shannon, Weaver, and the Minotaur: Redundancy in Language and Information Systems

Introduction

The legend of Theseus, known principally through *Plutarch's Life of Theseus* (Plutarch 100), is extraordinarily rich in instances of non-verbal graphic communication. Aegeus, King of Athens, and Aethra conceive Theseus at Troezen, Aegeus departs and leaves "a sword and a pair of sandals hidden under a great rock" as tokens to be given to the child, if it is a boy. When Theseus's childhood is past, he collects the tokens, travels to Athens, and deliberately reveals the sword to Aegeus as a clue to his identity. Recognition immediately follows (Plutarch 100: 15-20). Theseus's journey by land to Athens was a dangerous one and he encountered various difficulties and highwaymen on the way. The most appealing and appalling encounter might be with Procrustes, who trimmed or stretched travelers to fit his bed (the source for the idea of a Procrustean argument), and whose actions could be regarded as proleptic of indexing schemes to which documents are awkwardly assimilated.

The tokens carried by Theseus are primarily for the preservation of information over time, and, when carried over space, are known to the messenger, not bypassing his memory. There is a contrast here with the better-known episode of Bellerophon, recounted in the *Iliad*, who carried over space a sealed message whose contents were unknown to him and which were to endanger him (Warner 1994: 47-52). The relation of such forms of graphic communication to spoken language is not clear or agreed.

Received and recognized in Athens, and nominated as successor to Aegeus, Theseus set out for Crete to kill the Minotaur and prevent further payment of human tribute. The frequency of pictorial representations of the conflict with the Minotaur suggests that is a central episode. The Minotaur was concealed within a labyrinth and Theseus's return path traced through a thread suggested and supplied by Ariadne, the daughter of Minos, King of Crete. Ariadne's thread subsequently became a widely used metaphor for tracing a path through a labyrinthine argument. After killing the Minotaur, Theseus returned to Athens, abandoning Ariadne. The festival of Cybernesia, or the Pilot's festival, is said to be held in honor of the pilots of the ship by one source cited by Plutarch. The name *Cybernesia* anticipates the deliberate naming of various fields, "the study of language . . . the study of messages as a means of controlling machinery and society, the development of computing machines, and other such automata, certain reflections upon psychology and the nervous systems, and a tentative new theory of scientific method," as *cybernetics* by Wiener (1954).

The narrative given by Plutarch is not entirely internally consistent with regard to the literacy of the actors in the narrative, first understanding literacy in the sense of communication by written language. For instance, in one version, identified as "very singular" by Plutarch, is a reference to a forged letter brought to Ariadne, supposedly written by Theseus (Plutarch 100: 26-27). Such internal inconsistencies could be traced to the variety of sources cited by Plutarch and to the accretion of material associated with myth. In this respect, there is some formal comparability with the *Iliad* and the *Odyssey*: it has been suggested that the cultural portrait offered by Homer is best regarded as a conflation of accounts originating at different periods (Kirk 1985). A comparable, although not identical, relation to literacy does also emerge from the *Iliad* and the *Odyssey*: there is a variety of graphic communication, sophisticated forms of oral discourse, and a slightly fuller anticipation of forms regarded as written language (Warner 1994: 47-52). Theseus is usually dated to the generation before the Trojan War. At that period, Athens did not have written language, although Mycenean Crete had developed Linear B (Gaur 1992: 69-70). In a second, less restricted, sense of literacy—the ability to comprehend those message systems a culture considers important—the actors of the narrative had access to sophisticated forms of oral discourse and to a variety of graphic communication.

The instances of graphic communication are valuable as reminders that primarily oral societies did have forms of communication not necessarily linked to utterance. Nor are these forms of graphic signification iconic in the sense of there being a visual resemblance between signifier and signified. The sometimes presumed historical priority of iconic signs is further brought into question (see chapter 6). Considering these and other examples of graphic communication also diminishes the sense of radical novelty attached to recent or current innovations in information technology (Warner 1994).

Legends such as those of Theseus have an informative function in primarily or strongly oral societies, particularly for the communal preservation of information over time (Herodotus 430 BC; Vico 1744; Havelock 1982: 136). To stigmatize such episodes as mythical or fictional, rather than historical, would be to import a value judgment foreign to its original context. A distinction between myth and history may not be made by cultures without written language (Goody and Watt 1963: 47). The development of history has been taken to depend on the possibility of written recording of testimony (Biber 1988: 3). Herodotus, simultaneously regarded as the "father of lies" and the first historian, although both judgments can be tempered by a consideration of his intellectual context (Burn 1972), was concerned to ensure survival for oral traditions by collecting and transcribing them (Herodotus 430 BC: 178, 494; Warner 1994: 47-52). Plutarch, as a historian embedded in literacy, makes some initial reservations on the truth of the narrative, but he, concedes its fascination while carefully distinguishing different sources. Myth can be read historically (Vico 1744) and this chapter is itself partially prompted by a historical reading of a specific legend.

Theseus-Aegeus Code

One incident from the "Life of Theseus" should fascinate anyone familiar with the history of information science: the code arranged between Theseus and Aegeus.

> Aegeus [Theseus's father] gave the pilot a second sail, a white one, and ordered him on the return voyage to hoist the white canvas if Theseus were safe, but otherwise to sail with the black as a sign of mourning.
>
>   . . .
>
> The story goes that as they approached the shore of Attica Theseus was so overcome by joy that he forgot, and so, too did his pilot, to hoist the sail which was to signal their safe return to Aegeus and he in despair threw himself down from the cliff and was killed.

(Plutarch 100: 27-28)

The more immediately apparent points of interest are finally of marginal relevance to the themes to be developed, but they can be considered. Binary coding, embodied here in the contrast between a black and white sail, has been considered to be the minimal difference necessary for the construction of signification. It has been discovered in other contexts: for instance, the Congo talking drum is sometimes cited as one of the more arcane binary codes (*Encyclopaedia Britannica* 1910; Cherry 1957: 35; Finnegan 1970). The black sail does have symbolic value through its associations with mourning, and this value is present in the narrative, but, although this connection may reinforce the message, it is not essential to it. In one version, also recounted by Plutarch, the white sail is replaced by a scarlet one. Yet a binary contrast, with a prearranged code, would have been sufficient, without symbolic values. It could be said that we have signs that are simultaneously motivated, in the sense that there is a culturally recognized association between the signifier and what it signifies, but one that is potentially arbitrary.

The full fascination of the episode is revealed when it is placed in relation to the code model of communication given in *The Mathematical Theory of Communication* (Shannon and Weaver 1949). The crucial correspondences can be enumerated with a brief commentary:

- The agreement between Theseus and Aegeus corresponds to the establishment of the code linking sender and receiver, or addresser and addressee. In this case, the code is a narrative event, not a necessary hypothesis. The question of the origin of the code and the possibility of infinite regress, which has been seen as a weakness in this model of communication, does not arise. Interactive oral communication is also, in this instance, a precondition for the coded communication, not something that can necessarily be explained by it.

- Theseus corresponds broadly to the information source and Aegeus to the receiver. It should be recalled that the information source selects a message from the set of possible messages and converts it into a signal for transmission along a communication channel to a receiver.

- The messages, in abbreviated form, would be *safe* or *mourning*.

- The black or white sail corresponds to the signal.

- The communication channel could be identified as the visual link between Aegeus and Theseus.

(see Figure 1)

In the code model of communication, redundancy in signals is regarded as potentially valuable in counteracting the possible corrupting effects of noise in the communication channel. In this instance, we are concerned with a signal system without redundancy and the crucial misinterpretation that can be connected with its absence from the message. Corruption of the signal does not come directly from noise in the communication channel, but from Theseus' or the pilot's distraction.

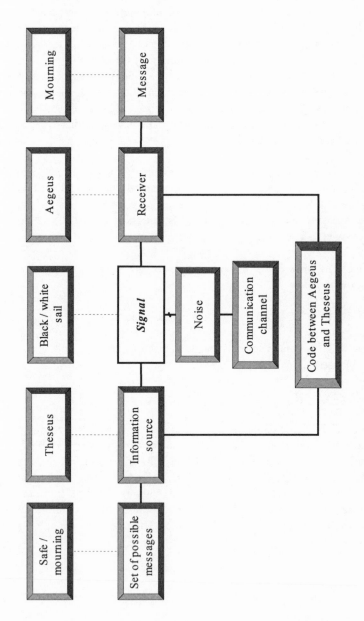

Figure 1. Code model and Theseus - Aegeus communication

A similar motif recurs in the later Tristan legend, where, in one version at least, the signal is subject to deliberate misreporting rather than accidental confusion (Warner 1994: 29). In contrast to the legend of Theseus, the episode occurs in the context of a society literate in the sense that some actors in the narrative also communicate by written language. Both communities in which the myths were sustained had access to a sophisticated, if potentially unreliable, non-verbal signaling system. The parallel between the narratives is valuable for reinforcing the sense that the misinterpretation is a crucial aspect of the episode.

The episode is of most interest in the legend of Theseus, in the context of a society not literate in the sense of using written language. The question can then be posed: Why should this form of communication over space have been followed by the adoption of a graphic communication system, which we can now regard as alphabetic written languages, so strongly marked by its redundancy? The thesis can be outlined in advance. It is known to be possible informally to grasp some of the principles of information theory, of *The Mathematical Theory of Communication*, without acquaintance with the formally developed theory. The devisers of alphabetic writing may, then, have deliberately incorporated redundancy to preserve the meaning of messages transmitted over space. Understanding the reasons for redundancy in written language may help understand why *The Mathematical Theory of Communication* has been simultaneously so successful in the analysis of written communication for such purposes as compression, whether for transmission or storage, and so unproductive, although tempting and influential, as a theoretical basis for information science.

Significance and Development of the Code Model

The code model of communication, as it is sometimes known, has been widely disseminated. It does not originate with *The Mathematical Theory of Communication* and can be reproduced and further disseminated without reference to this or other sources. Even when this source is cited, some of the reservations made by Shannon and Weaver can be ignored: for instance, Sperber and Wilson in *Relevance: Communication and Cognition* reproduce the diagram, citing Shannon and Weaver, without fully noticing the disclaimer that the theory does not deal directly with the semantic aspects of communication (Sperber and Wilson 1986: 4-5). A loss of subtle, although still significant, qualifications can be a common phenomenon in diffusion.

There is also some ambivalence in Shannon and Weaver's account in *The Mathematical Theory of Communication,* which may have encouraged the loss or erosion of the reservation that the theory does not deal directly with semantic aspects of communication. In frequently cited passages, Shannon and Weaver simultaneously distinguish the scope of their theory, but they express optimism as to its wider applicability.

> The mathematical theory of the engineering aspects of communication
> . . . admittedly applies in first instance to the . . . technical problems of
> the accuracy of transference of a signal from sender to receiver [but
> the theory has a deep significance and, although information is not to
> be confused with meaning, this does not imply] that the engineering
> aspects are necessarily irrelevant to the semantic aspects.
>
>   . . .
>
> entropy not only speaks the language of arithmetic; it also speaks the
> language of language.

(Shannon and Weaver 1949: 6, 8, and 28)

Those who can sense the clarity, elegance, and scope of this theory, even if they can only imperfectly understand its full mathematical development, will understand this optimism.

Subsequent critiques have reduced the optimism for the applicability of the theory to semantic levels. Bar-Hillel in "An examination of information theory" famously described *The Mathematical Theory of Communication* as a theory of signals, not information. This can be regarded as a more emphatic restatement of Shannon and Weaver's distinction of the engineering from the semantic aspects of information. Bar-Hillel does not accept the applicability of measures of information as measures of meaning or semantic content (and claims that Shannon explicitly disassociated himself from those who interpreted his measures of information in this way). However, in a not unfamiliar transformation, Bar-Hillel then goes on to substitute a different model for measuring semantic information, which could be criticized as equally artificial (Bar-Hillel 1955).

Colin Cherry, in *On Human Communication*, gave a very clear warning about extension of concepts of information theory encountered.

> These concepts [of information rate, channel capacity and equivocation] are not easy to acquire, nor simple to apply correctly. They are essentially mathematical and, what is most important, they are primarily of application to certain technical problems (mainly in telecommunication) under clearly defined conditions. It is only too easy and tempting to use these terms vaguely and descriptively, especially in relation to human communication–'by analogy'. The concepts and the methods of communication theory demand strict discipline in their use.

> (Cherry 1957: 198)

And Cherry did not follow Bar-Hillel in substituting a different theory.

A particularly valuable distinction for the purposes here that can still be recovered from Bar-Hillel's critique is between phonemic and semantic redundancy. Phonemic redundancy would refer to the greater number or variety of phonemes with which to differentiate the message unambiguously from other possible messages; semantic redundancy to elements of repetition or reinforcement of meaning in the original message. In the context of questioning a simple representational relation between written and spoken language, the term *phonemic* does have unwanted connotations that might be taken to imply a representative and unambiguous relation between phonemes, minimal units of significance in spoken language, and written characters. The distinction of phonemic from semantic redundancy still helps to distinguish the level of redundancy with which we are here concerned, with redundancy at level of expression and not content. At the level of expression with regard to written characters, it is possible further to distinguish mosaic redundancy from the extent to which letters differ from one another as potentially superimposed patterns (Cherry 1957:

291). In this context, the analysis stops short at the level of the individual character or letter and is not concerned with mosaic redundancy in differentiation of characters. However, it is at least acknowledged that what constitutes an individual character and the number of characters in an alphabet is not necessarily self-evident.

Although phonemic and semantic redundancy can be distinguished, there may be a similar cause or explanation for their existence, which has been called removal from direct semantic ratification (Ong 1982: 47). Direct semantic ratification is understood as the possibility of direct interrogation of the producer of a statement and of immediate acquaintance with its social or spatial context. Writing that draws on oral models can be used as a substitute for the presence of a live speaker, possibly open to questioning. Assertions in written language tend to be protected from the immediate questioning often possible with unrecorded speech. If writing is transmitted over space as well as time, the opportunity for acquaintance with its original context is liable to be diminished. For published documents, as distinct from correspondence, the opportunity of immediate dialogue with the producer tends to be greatly reduced. When a message is divorced from its spatial and social context, redundancy may assist in reconstructing the message both at the semantic and, crucially, at the level of expression.

Informal Grasping of Information Theory

There is evidence that some elements of information theory can be descriptively or informally grasped, without knowledge of the formally developed model. For instance, preexisting coding systems could be economic in assigning the shortest or most easily produced symbols to the most frequently occurring symbols or sequences in the communication to be encoded. Morse, for instance, visited a printer's office in order to establish the relative frequency of letter and he assigned the shortest codes to the most frequently occurring letters in ordinary written English. This has been regarded as a purely descriptive appreciation of a proposition comparable with the formalized idea in information theory that symbols with a high probability of occurrence convey little information (Cherry 1957: 36-37). Pitman's shorthand has also been regarded as a mapping of a hyperbolic to rectangular distribution of symbols (Lynch 1977).

In contrast, redundancy in written language would seem to have been treated as a given, not as something demanding explanation. For instance, although Pitman's shorthand may expose redundancy in written English, this had not led to attempts to explain it. It is difficult to determine reasons for the absence of questioning or explanation, but some influences can be strongly suggested. For scholarly discussions, the classic Aristotelian position which regards written language as a secondary representation of speech is one plausible influence: it has reduced the attention given to the internal dynamics of writing and encouraged seeking explanations for its structure in the correspondence with speech (Harris 1986). In extra-scholarly contexts, modern Western literacy also involves the integration in consciousness of speech and writing.

The integration in consciousness of speech and writing may also have been partially disturbed by changes in the relative communicative possibilities of spoken and written language since the mid-nineteenth century. Recorded or transmitted speech has partly usurped functions previously largely reserved to writing. Written language once had communicative possibilities denied to speech, the transmission of messages to receivers distant in space and time without immediate reliance on the memory of a human intermediary. The late-nineteenth-century inventions of the telephone (1876) and phonograph (1857-1877) enabled speech to be used for distant geographic and temporal communication. In turn, these audio media have been supplemented by audiovisual media, such as film and television, which can combine utterance and image for distant communication. The displacement of written language by recorded or transmitted speech for distant communication is sometimes described as secondary orality in contradistinction to the primary orality of societies without written language (Ong 1982). It has been accompanied by a reexamination of the relation of written to spoken language (Warner 1994).

The period since the late-nineteenth century has also witnessed the growth of scripts not directly intended as communicative substitutes for speech, designed for both commercial and scholarly purposes. In a commercial context, scripts such as telegraph codes, which function as ciphers for written language rather than direct substitutes for speech, have been developed. For scholarly purposes, increasingly sophisticated logical notations have supplemented and displaced the diagrams and verbal sentences used to give form to logical propositions. Computer programming languages can themselves be regarded as non-verbal forms of writing. For the purposes of claims to intellectual property, telegraphic codes, shorthand, and computer programming languages have all been regarded as forms of writing, particularly in a United Kingdom context, with partly similar but also contrasting patterns in the United States (see chapter 5). These forms of writing may remain susceptible to pronunciation, often by analogy with alphabetic written languages: but susceptibility to pronunciation cannot be assumed of other graphic forms possibly regarded as writing, particularly with regard to the synchronic interpretation of forms existing prior to the development of alphabetic written language.

It is possible, then, to disassociate forms of writing, including alphabetic writing, from speech and to consider them purely as graphic communication systems. Even if the writing is read to speech at reception or inception, or strongly associated with spoken language in consciousness, it remains subject to the constraints of graphic communication. In the reference to the constraints of graphic communication, some careful positive use of the code model for communication is being made.

Alphabetic Writing as Distant Communication

A distinction can be made between forms of writing intended primarily for preservation over time and for transmission across space (Warner 1994: 16-44). Some significant accounts of the development of writing have argued that alphabetic writing was intended to be used for distant communication. Giambattista Vico's schema in *The New Science* is crucial:

all nations began to speak by writing, since all were originally mute . . .

The first language had been hieroglyphic, sacred or divine; the second, symbolic, by signs or by heroic devices; the third, epistolary, for men at a distance to communicate to each other the current needs of their lives.

(Vico 1744: 138-140)

Hieroglyphs have been found predominantly, although not necessarily exclusively, as monumental inscriptions, intended for the preservation of information over time as opposed to the transmission of messages across space. The signs in the "Life of Theseus" (Plutarch 100) correspond to the second or symbolic form of writing. The third stage of writing, epistolary, corresponds to alphabetic writing although also to other forms. With "men at a distance" or epistolary communication, the message is divorced from the messenger. Various forms of redundancy, including redundancy at the level of expression, may be needed to enable the message to be reconstructed away from the social context of origination and without the possibility of dialogue and questioning. Redundancy at the level of expression would also need to counteract noise in transmission, for instance, damage to the document transmitted.

Rousseau gives a comparable account in distinguishing different stages of writing: the third way of writing is to break the speaking voice into a given number of elementary parts:

This way of writing, which is ours, must have been invented by commercial peoples who, in travelling to various countries, had to speak various languages, which would have them to invent characters that could be common to all of them. This is not exactly to represent speech, but to analyse it.

(Rousseau 1755: 17)

Again, there is a stress on communication over space, although the message would not necessarily be separated from the messenger. The further suggestion that alphabetic writing developed in encounters with non-native languages has been reiterated in modern contexts (Harris 1986: 117).

There have been discontinuities in the study of writing and potentially relevant antecedents have not necessarily been fully acknowledged by modern studies. The fullest modern attempt at reconstruction of the origins of writing, or at least of the development of the alphabet, does not distinguish sufficiently time from space dimensions (Harris 1986; see chapter 1). However, the reconstruction of intentions of devisers of alphabetic writing does resemble the model of communication associated with *The Mathematical Theory of Communication*. There is no direct citation, although this does not exclude indirect influence, and the terminology is similar.

> [The] entire architecture of the alphabetic system rests of the application of these two principles of equipollence and free sequential combination.
>
> (Harris 1986: 115)

Equipollence can be understood as meaning not hierarchically or relationally ordered. One contrast would be with the system of Arabic numerals. Free sequential combination and equipollence can be regarded as strongly analogous to the assumptions of independence and equal value in *The Mathematical Theory of Communication*. The departure from free sequential combination in alphabetic written language, in which familiar combinations of letters recur, can be regarded as the addition of redundancy at the level of expression, enabling the reconstruction of the message when carried upon imperfect, possibly noisy, media to its reception.

Conclusion

The original question, prompted by a historical and semiotic reading of a mythic episode, has been addressed: why is redundancy in alphabetic written language. The question itself raised redundancy from a given into something demanding explanation. The strong possibility has been indicated that redundancy was deliberate, and then inherited and sustained. Even the received alphabetic principle of a correspondence between written characters and spoken sounds may itself reinforce the continuing presence of redundancy.

The further question of why the information theory of *The Mathematical Theory of Communication* should have been simultaneously successful in the analysis of written communication for compression, whether for transmission or storage, and yet unproductive as a theoretical basis for information science, can also be considered. It can be suggested that systems of writing can be decomposed along the lines of their construction, but that a condition common to the forms of writing so decomposed is unlikely to yield interesting discriminations between samples of writing at the semantic level. One revealing analogy would be with indexing itself, where it is known that a term common to all documents or objects to be indexed will not yield valuable or interesting discriminations between those objects.

The code model of communication has been retained as an explanatory device for certain, particularly spatially distant, forms of communication. Its scope, particularly its application to interactive oral communication, has been reduced. With regard to one culturally important, graphic communication system, namely, alphabetic written language, redundancy has been made an object of explanation. It has also been suggested that its presence can be traced to an informal or descriptive grasping of the value of redundancy in distant communication, not primarily or originally to a representative relation to the spoken word.

Chapter 3

Not the Exact Words . . . : Writing, Computing, and Exactness

Mr. Wopsle answered, "Those are not the exact words."

"Not the exact words!" repeated the gentleman, bitterly. "Is that the exact substance?"

"Yes," said Mr. Wopsle.

Charles Dickens. *Great Expectations.* 1861.

Introduction

The topic to be developed is writing, computing, and exactness. The themes to be developed will be made clearer after a discussion of the full context of the epigraph above:

"I read that just now," Mr. Wopsle pleaded.

"Never mind what your read just now, sir; I don't ask you what you read just now. You may have read the Lord's Prayer backwards, if you like—and, perhaps, have done it before to-day. Turn to the paper. No, no, no, my friend; not to the top of the column; you know better than that; to the bottom, to the bottom." (We all begin to think Mr. Wopsle full of subterfuge.) "Well? Have you found it?"

"Here it is," said Mr. Wopsle.

"Now follow that passage with your eye, and tell me whether it distinctly states that the prisoner said that he was instructed by his legal advisers wholly to reserve his defence? Come! Do you make that of it?"

Mr. Wopsle answered, "Those are not the exact words."

"Not the exact words!" repeated the gentleman, bitterly. "Is that the exact substance?"

"Yes," said Mr. Wopsle.

(Dickens 1861: 139)

The source of this quotation, *Great Expectations*, is not usually considered within information studies. It should be noted that Jaggers—"the gentleman"—is a lawyer who, elsewhere in the novel, shows concern at the harshness of the written law, and that Mr. Wopsle has been giving a dramatic reading of a newspaper report of a murder.

A number of contrasts between spoken and written language are implied in this quotation. Some of the characteristics indicative of the document read by Mr. Wopsle are specific to written language and do not have precise correlates in speech: for instance, the injunction to turn to the bottom and not to the top of a column and to follow a passage with the eye indicate the spatial and visual character of writing, which can be contrasted with the time-extended and audible character of speech. The allusion to reading the Lord's Prayer backwards also indicates a form of reading, of deliberate pronunciation or giving non-verbal oral correlates to written signs, difficult to obtain from oral discourse alone (although it might be possible to construct it from oral discourse, or from memory, once those oral forms have been made objects for analysis, isolated from their communicative context, by the influence of written language). The passage itself reports speech and its highly interactive form recalls the dialogue associated with orality in contrast to the monologue associated with writing. In addition, the pattern of question and answer is strongly reminiscent of cross-examination of witnesses.

In the context of contrasts between written and spoken language, the triple repetition of "exact" can be taken as a deliberate allusion to Bacon's famous apothegm: "Writing [maketh] an exact man." In the passage, exactness is first understood as a one-to-one correspondence between written and spoken forms—"Not the exact words"—and, second and more conclusively, as a correspondence in meaning—"the exact substance."

The fuller series of contrasts made by Bacon can be considered:

Reading maketh a full man; conference a ready man; and writing an exact man.

(Bacon 1597: 209)

First, it can be asked which of these characteristics is unique to the communicative activity with which it is associated by Bacon and which can be supplied, at least in part or to some extent, by other forms of communication. For instance, the fullness associated with reading might be obtainable from oral discourse, although there can be limitations on the time and space of sources. However, with technological developments in media for communication since the late nineteenth century, limitations on spatial communication have diminished. The readiness associated with conference or conversation can be glossed primarily as the ability to reply quickly and cogently. Analogues to this can be found in written discourse: for instance, scholarly communication can be regarded as a public conversation in print and other media (Wilson 1983) and readiness could be evinced in the process of assertion, review, and reply, although at a slower pace than in oral dialogue. Bacon distinguishes reading from writing, and he does not simply regard them as mirror-image processes. The exactness encouraged and enabled by writing would seem to be specific to that communicative form. Bacon's concern is with the literate individual within a literate society and these concerns must be distinguished from the historical transition from orality to literacy. Preliteracy should not be confused with illiteracy. Yet, in this instance, the exactness enabled by writing can be taken as a crucial enhancement, with a historical as well as individual reference not fully anticipated in primary orality. A more carefully qualified, and fuller, perspective would be to regard written language as extending the possibility of exactness from number and geometry to other domains of human discourse, for instance, enabling the careful definition in logic of man as a rational animal or featherless biped (Kneale and Kneale 1962).

Three related senses of exactness can be distinguished: precise replication over time, including the replication of verbal forms both written and spoken over time; the capacity to make subtle distinctions, although this is anticipated in primary orality; and the ability to impose systematic order and control upon complexity, although this can again be said to have been anticipated in primary orality, particularly in the narratives surviving from oral cultures. Bacon's own emphasis is on precise replication over time: "If a man write little, he had need have a great memory" (Bacon 1597: 209).

The principal themes of this chapter can now be anticipated. The exactness encouraged and obtainable from written language and other forms of graphic signification can be regarded as a crucial feature not fully anticipated in primary orality. The possibility of exactness is essential to the development of computing and can be seen to underlie the development of activities, often considered separately, of working computers, formal logic and mathematics, and the theory of computation. Computing intensifies the possibility of exactness (for instance, the precise comparison of verbal forms, including collation or close textual analysis) but also encourages fluidity and change (for instance, in overwriting of files, the close succession of variants of text files difficult to distinguish as discrete states, and the liberty of contribution to networked information). In some senses, these themes could be considered special cases of more familiar propositions: for instance, it has been suggested that we need a culture of acquaintance with one form of information technology to move on to or develop a further stage. The relation between writing and computing could be regarded as an exemplification, although a highly important if not over-arching exemplification, of this proposition. In addition, it is customary to come across assertions of a reversion to secondary orality, in which spoken language has acquired some of the characteristics associated with writing, such as permanency and evidential status (Ong 1982; Warner 1994). The loss of some of the exactness associated with writing and its increasing vulnerability to erasure and modification without a strong lingering trace could be regarded as an aspect of secondary orality, in this instance, of writing assuming conditions previously associated primarily with speech.

Exactness

Writing and Exactness

Replication over Time

With regard to exactness in the sense of precise replication of verbal forms over time, it should be noted that oral cultures do have a concept of replication or, more accurately, of continuity over time that is different from the literate concept of verbatim repetition. A quotation from a Yugoslav oral poet from the 1930s illustrates this:

> By Allah I would sing it just as I heard it . . . It isn't good to change or to add.

> (Lord 1960: 27)

Oral poetry was significant to the preservation of information over time in primarily oral cultures. Some types of oral poetry, such as genealogies, have been regarded as having functions analogous to those attributed to written constitutions and charters in literate societies. For oral poets, the process of composition was not distinct from that of performance. They did not have the concept of a fixed text existing prior to its instantiation in utterance, may not have been able to isolate the word as a feature of utterance, and tended to insist that their performances were unchanged. If they acquired the concept of a fixed text, the process of composition and performance tended to be disabled—an example of the destructive effect of exactness. Most significantly, when measured against literate standards of verbatim repetition, oral poems were discovered to change over time, in some cases, to reflect changes in current social relations (Lord 1960). However, to assess them by reference to verbatim repetition would be to import an alien distinction. It might be more sophisticated to say that the notion of an exact written text existing prior to its instantiation in utterance, or replication in writing, develops with the introduction of writing.

Plato's *Phaedrus* is also concerned with the replication or preservation of verbal forms over time:

> No intelligent man will ever dare to commit his thoughts to words, still less to words that cannot be changed, as is the case with what is expressed in written characters.

(Plato 400 BC: 138)

Fixity over time is explicitly seen as a characteristic of written words. Fluidity, associated with oral dialectic, is valued. The passage contrasts with the commonly held modern assumption that stability over time is an important feature of valid arguments. Plato's dialogues have also been read to reveal ambivalent attitudes to orality and literacy. In the *Phaedrus* objections to written language, particularly its inability to engage in dialogue like a live speaker, are made. Other Platonic dialogues give contrasting views (Harris 1989). The method of dialectic could be regarded as analogous to an oral dialogue, yet the insistence on formal, sharply delimited definitions and division of concepts has been associated with the influence of writing (Harris 1989).

Simple dichotomies between orality and literacy cannot be sustained. The written concept of replication is itself complex and there are continuities as well as contrasts between oral and written charters. A touchstone judgment in the development of United States copyright is relevant both to the idea of orality and literacy as a continuum, and, specifically, to the concept of the replication of verbal forms.

> [The Constitution does not] "embalm inflexibly the habits of 1789 . . . its grants of power to Congress comprise, not only what was then know, but what the ingenuity of men should devise thereafter." [The grant of the Constitution, here with regard to] "writings," [should be interpreted by] "the general practices of civilized peoples in similar fields."

(Reiss v. National Quotation Bureau 1921)

To regard the changes over time in oral charters as indicative of their mythological rather than their historical character could inhibit the perception of strongly analogous processes occurring with regard to written charters in literate societies. Form is distinguished from meaning in a way that does not seem to have been available in primary orality, and precise replication of the form is insisted upon, but the interpretation accorded to significant clauses in charters is continually changed. The injunction to interpret the Constitution in the light of "the general practices of civilized people in similar fields" could be regarded as strongly analogous to the way in which oral charters change over time (see also chapter 5). Although highly literate cultures may have relative agreed criteria for the replication of verbal forms— although even these should be made objects of investigation rather than being accepted as self-evident—the interpretation of written documents is continually being changed. Here can be sensed what has been described as the central paradox of writing, that its appearance of exactness is continually betrayed by the possibility of different interpretations (McKenzie 1990).

The central paradox of writing has been discovered in Bacon:

> There are more doubts that rise upon our statutes, which are a text law, than upon the common law, which is no text law.

> (Quoted in McKenzie 1990)

Common understandings, possibly orally communicated, can give rise to fewer disputes than explicit written clauses in legislation. There is a familiar contrast between the United States and the United Kingdom, which is relevant here, between a written constitution and a set of informal understandings.

Control of Complexity and Subtle Distinctions

Accounts of the origin of writing associate it with geometry and number.

> It was this king [Sesotris], moreover, who divided the land into lots and gave everyone a square piece of equal size, from the produce of which he exacted an annual tax. Any man whose holding was damaged by the

encroachment of the river would go and declare his loss before the king, who would send inspectors to measure the extent of the loss, in order that he might pay in future a fair proportion of the tax at which his property had been assessed. Perhaps this was the way in which geometry was invented, and passed afterwards into Greece—for knowledge of the sundial and the gnomon and the twelve divisions of the day came into Greece from Babylon.

(Herodotus 430 BC: 169)

Sources other than Herodotus also trace the origins of geometry to the need to recover boundaries obliterated by the rising of the Nile. Herodotus himself was concerned to ensure the survival of disappearing oral traditions by committing them to writing. The contrast between fluidity and exactness emerges in a peculiarly physical sense. In this context, it should be noted that exactness, in the sense of the ability to make precise distinction and to construct or analyze complex formations, is associated with, and obtainable from, graphic forms other than written language. It may even be difficult to give verbal equivalents to geometric distinctions, either in written or spoken language, without a loss of exactness or clarity. In relation to the initial themes of this chapter, we are beginning to deal with the development of an area of study, of geometry, indirectly associated with the development of computing.

Mathematical and logical notations have been regarded as enabling the construction of elaborate systems of reasoning:

Various collocations of symbols become familiar as representing important collocations of ideas; and in turn the possible relations— according to the rules of the symbolism—between these collocations of symbols become familiar, and these further collocations represent still more complicated relations between the abstract ideas. And thus the mind is finally led to construct trains of reasoning in regions of thought in which the imagination would be entirely unable to sustain itself without symbolic help. Ordinary language yields no such help.

(Whitehead and Russell 1913: 2)

Mathematics is sometimes cited as the paradigm case of a discipline whose development is crucially dependent upon the possibility of graphic representation (Harris 1986: 151). In this instance, we are not dealing with verbal language, either written or spoken, but with a notation for symbolic logic, although it should be recalled that the origins of formal logic are associated with the influence of written language (Harris 1989). The particular sense of exactness we are concerned with here is the ability to make and sustain subtle distinctions, although the idea of systematic control of complexity is also relevant. In other contexts, exactness has emerged as an impediment, for instance, in the disabling of oral poets; and with regard to mathematics, there can be a conflict between lucidity and notational correctness.

The quotation from the *Principia Mathematica* is also intriguing because of the significance of its concluding point: that the "mind is finally led to construct trains of reasoning in regions of thought in which the imagination would be entirely unable to sustain itself without symbolic help." *Symbolic* in this context refers to the notation of formal or symbolic logic used in the *Principia Mathematica*. The passage continues: "Ordinary language offers no such help." The distinction between "ordinary language" and a logical symbolism is analogous to a distinction of the object from the metalanguage of formal or symbolic logic, although Whitehead and Russell may not have been fully aware of the possibility of a systematic formulation of this distinction (Ramsey 1926a). There is a contrast with the position formally endorsed by Whitehead and Russell that would tend to insist that the entities described by symbolic logic exist independently of the notational resources for describing them. This contrast need not be raised to the status of a logical contradiction.

Mathematics can also be observed to betray patterns analogous to those observed with written charters in literate societies, in which the form is fixed while the interpretation is changed. This has been regarded as a classic move in the development of mathematics.

And in thus preserving the form while modifying the interpretation, I am following in the great school of mathematical logicians, who, in virtue of a series of startling definitions, have saved mathematics from the sceptics, and provided a rigid demonstration of its propositions.

(Ramsey 1926a: 219)

The reference to a "rigid demonstration of its propositions" can be read as exemplifying exactness in the sense of the ability to make and sustain precise distinctions.

Computing and Exactness

Construction of the Computer As a Machine

It is arguable that without the possibility for precise discrimination and the systematic control of complexity offered by graphic signification, the physical artifact of the computer could not have been constructed. The exactness obtainable from writing and other forms of graphic signification, such as diagrams, would seem to have been an essential preliminary to the construction of computers as machines. The construction of working computers and the development of computational theory were, in part, separate developments. Formal logic and mathematics, from which context computational theory emerged, have been revealed as strongly dependent on graphic representation for their development. In contrast to the citation of mathematics as a discipline crucially dependent on the possibility of graphic representation, the importance of writing and graphic signification to the construction of computers as machines would seem to have received little notice. The development of logic and systematic methods of enquiry and analysis has occasionally been recognized as an essential precursor to their construction: "without the systematic analysis that Boolean methods make possible, the construction of large-scale digital computers would be virtually unthinkable" (Davis 1988: 319). This is an isolated remark whose implications are not fully explored. However, it does indicate that writing, and particularly the exactness associated with writing, could constitute a crucial element linking the development of mathematics, formal logic, and automata theory to the construction of the computer as machine (Warner 1994).

Capacity for Enhanced Exactness

Computer applications can enable enhanced exactness. For instance, with regard to the precise replication of verbal forms over time, close comparisons (equivalent to an extensive bibliographic collation) can be made, with greater ease than could be obtained from printed sources alone. Variants of a file can be collated and changes revealed. In the sense of exactness as control of complexity, it may be possible to arrive at a more precise estimate of the number of records in a large catalogue when it is converted from printed to electronic form. This sense of exactness is also revealed in an early comment on mechanical mathematics: the logician Hao Wang noted that machines can bypass human limitations on comprehending great masses of detail and suggested that it would be interesting if the machine discovers mistakes in the *Principia Mathematica*. An example of the discovery of such an error, in the particular sense of the detection by a computer program of redundancy in the existing reasoning, is given (Wang 1960). The processes of discovery in these instances could themselves be regarded as examples of the intensification of the possibilities of exactness by computing. They may also enforce a recognition that what has been regarded as exact is less self-consistent than was thought. It might be possible to find other examples of computing, and other information technologies, intensifying the possibility of exactness and revealing the presence of fluidity or change in what was regarded as precise. For instance, the replication of spoken words has been revealed as perceptual, not physical. (See also chapter 6: "Review of Samuel Johnson. *A Dictionary of the English Language on CD-ROM*").

Increased Fluidity

Computer applications may simultaneously enable or encourage, although they need not compel, greater fluidity. It would not be difficult to adduce examples of the computer-based treatment of written language, which betray characteristics of fluidity and change, previously associated primarily with spoken language. The liberty of written contribution to networked information can be considered: in the case of a lightly moderated discussion list, public written communication is assuming the conditions of an oral conversation, of rapid interchange and response. Similarly, with frequently revised text files, there is no direct equivalent to possibly discrete successive drafts, and, if made public, are not necessarily a precise analogue to successive printed editions. The very rapidity of change may weaken the analogy to successive editions, even if successive variants are identifiable. With a computer-held database changed at frequent intervals, it has become difficult to isolate precise analogues to successive editions of a printed text for the purposes of copyright. In its continual change and preservation by renewal, a computer-held database can be regarded as analogous to the sustained but continually changing forms of discourse found in primary orality. Yet there is also a contrast. The computer-held database text is now identified as changing, not perceived as invariant, by its contrast with the idea of a fixed text produced in relatively discrete successive editions and inherited from a print-based culture.

Value of Exactness

What has been the value attached to exactness? One strong, if not dominant, literate tradition has been to value exactness, to insist on precise discriminations, to be reluctant to work with terms that are poorly understood or insufficiently defined. Geometry, for instance, has been taken as an exemplar or model for forms of thought to be followed in other disciplines (Ryle 1949). Yet even with Aristotle, with his insistence on precise definitions and categorizations, we can find reservations on the level of precision legitimately to be expected from discussions.

> Our account of this science [politics] will be adequate if it achieves such clarity as the subject-matter allows; for the same degree of precision is not to be expected in all discussions, any more than in all the products of handicraft . . . it is a mark of the trained mind never to expect more precision in the treatment of any subject than the nature of that subject permits; for demanding logical demonstrations from a teacher of rhetoric is clearly about as reasonable as accepting mere plausibility from a mathematician.

(Aristotle 323 BCa: 64-65)

The early association, here partly implied, between mathematics and logical demonstration, should also be noted.

A less-dominant, but appealing, tradition has been to place reservations on the value of exactness and the extent of the applicability of logical and mathematical method to human affairs. Radical objections to the scope of logical method can be found in the work of philosopher Giambattista Vico:

> Young men who have devoted much time to algebra find themselves later, to their great dismay and regret, less apt in the affairs of civil life.

(Vico 1725: 125)

> Truly, if you were to apply the geometrical method to practical life 'you would no more than spend your labor on going mad rationally' and you would drive a straight furrow through the vicissitudes of life as if whim, rashness, opportunity, and luck did not dominate the human condition. To compose a public address according to the geometric method would be the same as excluding everything clever from it.

(Vico 1710: 98-99)

Readers may wish to consider the degree of congruence between these observations and their own biographical experience.

Conclusion

In summary, this chapter has argued: that the exactness obtainable from writing and other forms of graphic signification was a cultural feature not fully anticipated in primary orality; that various senses of exactness can be distinguished; that the possibility of exactness was crucial to the development of logic, mathematics, and the construction of the computer as a machine; and that developments associated with computing have both intensified the possibilities of exactness and encouraged fluidity and change, including revealing existing human semiotic constructions as less self-consistent than they had been received. The approach to the influence of medium of communication has been non-deterministic, in a deliberate contrast with technological determinism. From this perspective, the medium can enable or even encourage, but need not compel, certain forms of communicative practice.

Returning to Bacon's observation that, "conference [maketh] a ready man; writing an exact man," it may be recalled that scholarly communication could be regarded as a conversation in print and, increasingly, other media. This chapter, previously delivered as that specialized form of oral communication, the lecture or conference paper, approaching a monologue and drawing on graphic support, can now become part of a wider public discussion in the hope that responses will remain informed by an oral spirit and not written strictness.

Chapter 4

Toward an Integrated Account of Formal Logic and Automata Theory: Iconic and Notational Models

Introduction

Giving a widely intelligible account of the primitive logical operations associated with the computer and of the limits of the computational process is first complicated by the variety of programming languages, heterogeneity of programs as socially produced artifacts, and consequentially wide range of meanings acquired by the term *program*. Real-world complexity and difficulties over definition can be avoided, without loss of generality, by recourse to automata theory. It provides models that can be correlated with a program, data, and a computer. Most significantly, understanding the computational process through an abstract model can yield a grasp of fundamental matters that could never be obtained while "immersed in inessential detail and distraction" and that can then be brought back to the practical world (Minsky 1967: 2-3). Yet the depth and clarity of understanding of the computational process that can be obtained from automata theory is limited by its distance from working computers and formal logic.

Automata theory can be used to provide a model for the human computational process, for programs, data, and working computers. Its modern development can be traced from mathematical logic in the 1930s and was, at least in some respects, separate from the development and construction of working computers. Most memorably, it has been observed: "Logic [and automata theory] was a bastard of mathematics and philosophy; while actual computers first came into being as a great feat of engineering." (Wang 1974: 292) Distinctions have tended to persist and a curious mixture of mystical practice and restrained theory has been observed (Leith 1990: 115). An integrated account of automata theory and working computers, although valuable and desirable, is not easily obtained.

The distance between automata theory and working computers could be reduced by a perspective that insists that information technologies are human constructions (Warner 1999). The computer, and other information technologies, can be regarded as the congealed product of communal human labor, *"organs of the human brain, created by the human hand*; the power of knowledge, objectified" (Lyotard 1984: 86; Marx 1873: 706). The human capacities for constructing systems of signs and complex technological artifacts has given rise to information technologies that can be regarded as precursors of and, in some respects, enabling preliminaries for the computer. For instance, the introduction of written language to the Greek world witnessed the development of those analytic activities subsequently differentiated as formal logic and grammar, which were to be significant to the development of the theory of computation (Warner 1994: 55 and 114). Francis Bacon famously observed, "writing [maketh] an exact man" (Bacon 1985: 209), and without the exactness and systematic control of complexity obtainable from writing and other forms of graphic signification the construction of the computer as machine would seem difficult, if not impossible.

A comparative reading also suggests that automata theory has been a partly separate activity from formal logic and mathematics, although there would seem to have been less public recognition of this contrast. The contrast also assumes a different form. In this case, there is not an easily recognizable distinction between the mathematical constructions embodied in abstract automata and the construction of a material object. Rather there is a more subtle and elusive contrast between two different modes of representation favored by intersecting, although not unified, thought communities. Diagrammatic forms tend to be preferred for automata and notational forms for formal logic (See Figures 1 and 2). A unified account of automata theory and formal logic, although

^	and
v	or
~	not
->	If ... then
<->	If, and only if, ... then
|	Sheffer stroke (see p. 65 for a reading)
□	There exists
(χ)	For all χ
Φ	Greek phi used for a propositional function

These logical symbols can be given verbal correlates, as indicated. However, these verbal readings should be understood as informal renderings which may initially aid understanding and not as final or precise interpretations.

equally desirable, remains elusive.

Three broadly distinguishable and particularly significant strands associated with the study of the computational process can, then, be detected: automata theory, formal and mathematical logic, and working computers. They do not seem to have been fully integrated with one another. Even texts that treat computers, automata theory, and formal logic (Wang 1974; Herken 1995; Penrose 1989), or automata theory and formal logic (Davis 1982; Boolos and Jeffrey 1989), do not provide an integrated account.

The intention here is to indicate the possibility of developing an integrated account of automata theory and formal logic. A discussion of automata theory raises acute problems of cognitive authority and purpose and level of exposition. Cognitive authority with regard to automata studies has tended to be implicitly claimed by discursive communities associated with mathematical logic and computer science. The argument here is not with their competence within that domain but with any implied claim to exclusive proprietorship over that domain. The approach here aims to respect claims to competence within the domain by observing the required formalities, but not to concede exclusive proprietorship over that domain.

With regard to automata studies, there is an apparent congruence between mathematical and ordinary discourse concepts. Discussions recognize that formal models for computability coincide in their computational power with what are regarded as intuitive notions of computability (Boolos and Jeffrey 1989: 20; Sommerhalder and Westrhenen 1988: 32-33). The central concept of automata studies, of computability, is regarded as intuitively given and not open to formal proof (Minsky 1967: 105). More sophisticatedly, it could be regarded as culturally formed and historically developed, but still widely shared. Cultural influences for its wide dissemination might include pedagogic inculcation of methods of calculation, themselves partly associated with the exactness offered by graphic signification.

The relevance of the possibility of an integrated account of automata theory and formal logic to information science should be readily grasped. In terms of the thesis that being determines consciousness, information science has convincingly been seen as a partly unreflexive response to developments in telecommunications and computing from the late 1940s (Brown 1987). Intellectual effort expended within information science on comprehending and assimilating developments that have proved less productive than anticipated, such as expert systems and neural networks, can be partly traced to an inadequate understanding of the computational process. The semiotic perspective, which will be adopted here, has been increasingly influential in information science since the early 1990s (Warner 1990; Buckland 1997; Mai 1997).

Automata studies

Automata studies, in the modern sense intended here of formal models of the computational process, can be traced to seminal papers published in the 1930s[1]. Different definitions of effective calculability and models of the computational process were made public by lecture or written publication in 1935 and 1936 by Church, Kleene, Turing, and Post (Church 1936; Kleene 1935; Post 1936; Turing 1937). A degree of intellectual convergence has been detected (Gandy 1995). Some direct mutual influences, for instancem, from Church to Post (Davis 1965: 289), are also known to have existed, although these are difficult to trace and to isolate from the embracing intellectual context, particularly with regard to purely oral exchanges. The definitions and models are considered to be equivalent in computational power.

The models of the computational process made public in 1936 were not necessarily labeled as automata at the time of their initial dissemination (Post 1965; Turing 1937). They seem rather to have emerged from a concern with formalizing the computational process and with the *Entscheidungsproblem*, whether there could be a general effective procedure for determining the equivalence of two well-formed formulas of a formal system. For mathematical formalism, the process of computation was analyzed as consisting of the writing, erasure, and substitution of symbols, according to given rules (Ramsey 1926: 164-166). The definitions and models made public in 1935 and 1936 could be regarded as a further formalization of this analysis.

Although the different definitions and models developed by Church, Kleene, Post, and Turing are acknowledged to be equivalent in computational power, there may be difficulties in encoding from one model to another. Here, then, is a trace of the difficulties that can arise from finally commensurable, but not easily compatible, notations. From the current historical perspective, the models formulated by Church, Kleene, and Post can be regarded as of largely historical interest, once their formal equivalence has been noted.

The subsequent development of automata studies has witnessed a conflict between realism, in the sense of increasing resemblance between the model and working computers, and preservation of simplicity. Different models for the computational process do share a commonality of significant features. Models characteristically involve: (i) a sequence of machine or calculation states; (ii) a symbol space for reading, writing, and erasure; and (iii) a prescribed alphabet of symbols permitted in the symbol space. The sequence of logical operations, which can include change of machine or calculation state, writing, or erasing symbols and movement with the symbol space, is determined by the current state and the symbol read. The symbol space can either be deliberately restricted or unlimited. Finite automata are accordingly distinguished from growing and from infinite automata[2] (Minsky 1967: 13). The accepted conclusion is that different models for infinite automata yield equivalent sets of computable functions (Boolos and Jeffrey 1989: 19-20). This conclusion might be explained by the commonality of significant features shared by different models, although discussions of automata seem seldom to explore this possibility. There is no limit to alternative formulations of computability. Attention can, then, be turned to the Turing machine model, thereby acknowledging the communicative value of a shared model.

Turing Machine Model

Turing's model for the computational process was at least partly derived from an analysis of the actions performed by a person in computing a number, or from the formalist account of this process: "We may compare a man in the process of computing a real number to a machine which is only capable of a finite number of conditions" (Turing 1937: 231). The derivation of the model from an account of the human computational process may be one source for an unfortunate ambiguity in Turing's discussion: the sequence of states assumed by the model are sometimes referred to as states of mind and also, less anthropomorphically, as a note of instructions (Turing 1937). This inconsistency would seem to be a possible source for the analogies between the computer and human brain or mind.

The Turing machine model for the computational process has tended to be given a dual function. First, in accord with its origin in mathematical logic, it has been used to establish the limits for mathematical formalism, although not to the exclusion of other approaches. Second, following the development of the stored program computer (1944), it has been used to avoid difficulties over the definition of a program and of a computer. Even when it is primarily used to avoid real-world complexity, examples of computational processes tend to be derived from mathematical, or more narrowly, numerical domains. Distinctions that can be made between these two uses of the Turing machine model, as a formalization of the computational process and a means of avoiding difficulties over the definition of a program and a computer, are, then, analytical, not necessarily substantive. Yet each aspect deserves separate, if summary, consideration before moving on to a consideration of the logical operations associated with the Turing machine model.

In relation to mathematical formalism, the Turing machine model has been valued for its apparently objective character. Its apparent objectivity is contrasted with the merely relative definitions that can be obtained from a formal logic. A classic statement by Gödel encapsulates this distinction:

It seems that this importance [of Turing's computability] is largely due to the fact that with this concept one has for the first time succeeded in giving an absolute definition of an interesting epistemological notion, i.e., one not depending on the formalism chosen. In all other cases treated previously, such as demonstrability or definability, one has been able to define them only relative to a given language, and for each individual language it is clear that the one thus obtained is not the one looked for.

(Gödel 1946: 84)

One implied object of the contrast would be a formal system, such as that of the *Principia Mathematica,* where propositions distinguished as primitive and consequent are expressed in logical notation in the object-language and in written language in the metalanguage (Whitehead and Russell 1913) (compare Figures 1 and 2). The contrast made by Gödel between an absolute and linguistically relative definition would seem to have been since largely sustained. Acceptance of this dichotomy may have been one factor impeding the development of an integrated account of automata theory and formal logic. The main, although not exclusive, emphasis for mathematical formalism has tended to be on identifying domains that are not computable by purely formal procedures rather than on the possibility of formalizing domains that remain potentially computable (Herken 1995; Wang 1960; Beeson 1995).

A reiterated theme of automata studies is that a process is computable if, and only if, it is Turing machine computable and that modifications to Turing machines do not enlarge their computational power (Minsky 1967: 261; Davis 1982: 3; Bavel 1991). This has come to be known variously as *Church's thesis* (Boolos and Jeffrey 1989: 20), *Turing's thesis* (Rayward-Smith 1986: x; Shields 1987: 29) and the *Church-Turing thesis* (Penrose 1989: 47-49). The Church-Turing thesis will be the preferred term here. Although generally accepted, and considered not to have been falsified, it is not regarded as proven (Boolos and Jeffrey 1989: 20). It therefore provides an example of a proposition that is believed, although not considered proven, by the discursive communities claiming cognitive authority for formal logic and automata studies. Like the Turing machine model itself, it is placed outside established methods of formal proof, although there is a contrast between the treatment of the model and the thesis. The model tends to be regarded as an absolute account of the computational process, whereas the thesis is taken to appeal to intuition, to what would naturally be regarded as computable (Sommerhalder and Westrhenen 1988: 32).

Turing machine theory also reveals a consensus on the significant features of the Turing machine model. Significant characteristics cited are: a sequence of machine states, a symbol space, and an alphabet of symbols to be accepted in the symbol space. The Turing machine is capable of changing machine state and reading or writing symbols from the prescribed alphabet in the symbol space (see Figure 2). The alphabet of symbols can be reduced to a binary contrast between two different symbols, or a larger number of symbols can be permitted. The most significant variable elements in the Turing machine model are, then: the number of symbols in the alphabet, the extent of the symbol space, and the number of machine states. These exist in a broadly inverse relation: a restricted alphabet of symbols requires a greater number of machine states; and a small number of machine states can be compensated for by an expanded alphabet of symbols (Shannon and McCarthy 1956: 157-165). A Turing machine permitting an unrestricted number of machine states and an unrestricted symbol space, or a growing or infinite automaton, is considered more powerful than a machine with a restricted number of machine states or a finite automaton[3]. As the Church-Turing thesis implies, a restricted or expanded alphabet of symbols does not alter the computational power of the Turing machine, although it may facilitate clarity in presentation.

The set of significant features of a sequence of machine states, a symbol space, and an alphabet of symbols gives rise to a small, but still sufficient, set of logical operations associated with the Turing machine model. The sequence of logical operations can be interpreted as a series of condition: action clauses. Each condition is composed of a combination of current machine state and symbol read in the symbol space. An action can consist of the symbol to be written in the symbol space, or the direction of motion within the symbol space, and the next machine state.

The graphic forms and notation given to Turing machines has been less unified than either its themes or the significant features of the Turing machine model. Forms used include diagrams, often *labeled graphs* (Rayward-Smith 1986: xiii) (a mathematical form of representation analogous to, although not necessarily identical with, that conveyed by the more ordinary discourse terms *diagram* and *flow-chart*), or notational sequences with characters drawn from a specified, although not standardized, set. The lack of a common notation has been considered to have hampered the development of automata studies (Bavel 1991: viii).

A particular conflict in the notation used to represent the agreed characteristics of the Turing machine model can be between formality,

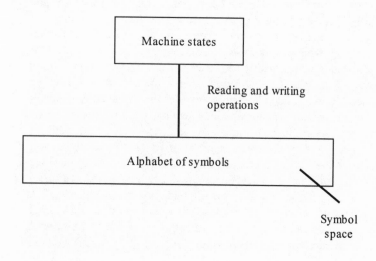

Figure 2. Significant characteristics of the Turing machine model

as required by the discursive communities who have claimed cognitive authority in automata studies, and clarity. For instance, the notation for the sequence of states, movements within the symbol space, and symbols read and written can be reduced to a binary contrast of 0 and 1, although this does not aid intelligibility. Alternatively, comprehension can be assisted by a notation with iconic elements: for instance, a sequence of states can be designated "$q1\ q2\ q3\ \ldots\ qn$," where "$q2\ q3$ $\ldots\ qn$" recall "$q1$" by a modified resemblance. A tension between formality and clarity is reported elsewhere in formal logic and mathematics: for instance, Whitehead and Russell concede that they have had to sacrifice notational lucidity to correctness at points in the *Principia Mathematica* (Whitehead and Russell 1913: 1). Some notations for Turing machines, together with their diagrammatic correlates, do manage to reconcile formality with clarity.

A notation that is both clear and formalized is used in a standard study of automata, *Computability and Logic* (Boolos and Jeffrey 1989), and their conventions can be indicated. Their Turing machine model, which resembles but it does not precisely replicate Turing's original model, is an infinite automaton: a calculating head, capable of assuming different machine or calculation states, moves above an unending tape divided into squares (see Figure 3). The sequence of states of the Turing machine is represented by characters drawn from the prescribed sequence, "$q1\ q2\ q3\ \ldots\ qn$." The alphabet of symbols to be accepted is limited to "0" and "1;" symbols to be written are similarly restricted; and the acts of reading and writing are denoted as "$s0$", when a "0" is read or written and "$s1$," when a "1" is written. No notational provision for erasure is made as this is subsumed in the act of overwriting. Symbols are read from, and written onto, the tape that corresponds to the symbol space commonly distinguished in models of the computational process. The direction of motion over the tape is denoted by "L" for left and "R" for right moves of the calculating head. The particular Turing machine is itself represented as a sequence of quadruples. Each quadruple is constituted by the current state of the Turing machine, symbol read, symbol to be written or direction of tape motion, and next state. A semicolon (;) is used to divide quadruples. The process of computation is taken to halt when no successor configuration occurs and this will be denoted by an incomplete quadruple (see Figure 4). In addition to these formalized elements, the following convention is observed: at the beginning of the computation, the head of the Turing machine will be in state q_1 positioned above the leftmost "1" of the input string, and at the end of the computation it will halt over the rightmost "1" of the output string[3] (see Figure 5).

Semiotic Aspects

Mathematics is often cited as the paradigm case of a discipline whose conceptual development has been crucially dependent on the possibility of graphic representation (Harris 1986: 152). The relation between mathematics and graphic representation holds true even at an elementary level (Goody 1977: 12). Similarly, even in computational processes of limited scope, a human calculator rapidly becomes a prisoner of the notation. At a more sophisticated and complex level, Whitehead and Russell remarked:

> Various collocations of symbols become familiar as representing important collocations of ideas; and in turn the possible relations— according to the rules of the symbolism—between these collocations of symbols become familiar, and these further collocations represent still more complicated relations between the abstract ideas. And thus the mind is finally led to construct trains of reasoning in regions of thought in which the imagination would be entirely unable to sustain itself without symbolic help.

> (Whitehead and Russell 1913: 2)

Whitehead and Russell continue: "Ordinary language yields no such help" (Whitehead and Russell 1913: 2).

Formal logic seems to be less frequently cited as a form of discourse crucially dependent on the possibility of graphic representation. Yet the thesis of Whitehead and Russell, that mathematics is reducible to logic, would seem to imply that their comments on the value of symbolism are equally applicable to formal logic as well (whether this continues to be accepted or not). An observation on the significance of notation to logic was made by Wittgenstein in the *Tractatus Logico-Philosophicus*: "It now becomes clear why we often feel as though "logical truths"

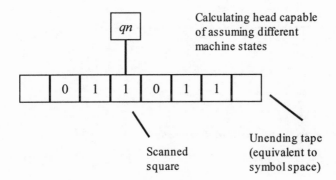

Machine states $= \{q1\ q2\ q3\ ...\ qn\}$

Alphabet of symbols $= \{01\}$

Figure 3. Turing machine model

Current states of calculating head	Symbol read	Symbol written or direction of motion of head	Next state of calculating head	Machine aspect
qn	s0 or s1	s0 or s1 or L or R	*qn*	Notational equivalent

Machine aspects and notational equivalents

*qn*s0s1*qn*;

Example of a complete quadruple

*qn*s0s1

Example of an incomplete quadruple

Figure 4. Notational conventions for the Turing machine

must be "postulated" by us. We can, in fact, postulate them in so far as we can postulate an adequate notation" (Wittgenstein 1922: 163). Although this remark is analogous to Whitehead and Russell's comments on the value of specialized symbolism to mathematics and logic, there is also a significant contrast: Whitehead and Russell seem, although only in part, to regard notation as something objectively given, analogous to the discovery of the Platonic universals denoted; rather, Wittgenstein emphasizes the human construction of the notational artifact. The notational systems constructed are intolerant of errors and vulnerable to collapse if modified:

> The introduction of a new expedient in the symbolism of logic must always be an event full of consequences. No new symbol may be introduced in logic in brackets or in the margin—with, so to speak, an entirely innocent face.

> (Wittgenstein 1922: 123)

The origin of logical systems as human artifacts does not, then, necessarily imply that they can be fully understood even by their immediate makers.

With less narrowly circumscribed universes of discourse, the conclusion might not be self-evidently readable from the input. Procedures may become so complicated that their results cannot be known with certainty prior to the analysis. Analysis itself can be subject to error. If formal logic is taken to consist of tautologies, its propositions may never surprise us (Wittgenstein 1922), but they may not have been fully anticipated.

Methodology of Construction

The method of elaboration of the Turing machine model from its concise formulation seems to have been anticipated in Vico's comments on the geometric method:

> The whole secret of the geometric method comes to this: first to define the terms one has to reason with; then to set up certain common maxims agreed to by one's companion in argument; finally, at need, to ask

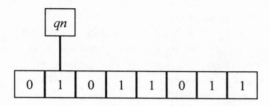

Starting state

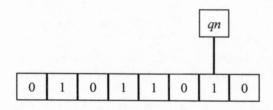

Halting state

Figure 5. Turing machine starting and halting states

discretely for such concessions as the nature of things permits, in order to supply a basis for arguments, which without some such assumption could not reach their conclusions; and with these principles to proceed step by step in one's demonstrations from simpler to more complex truth, and never to affirm the complex truths without first examining singly their component parts

(Vico 1725: 125-126).

For Vico, geometry and arithmetic differed only in the quantities they treated, not in their methods (Vico 1710: 156). Vico would differ significantly from Gödel's emphasis on the objective character of the Turing machine model in his insistence on the humanly constructed nature of any concise formulation, as well as its further elaboration, rather than receiving such models as objects of contemplation. An analogy can be drawn with the contrast between Whitehead and Russell's implicit suggestion that a notation is objectively given and Wittgenstein's emphasis that they are "postulated" by us.

A relation to the connectives of formal logic is implicit, rather than explicit, in the Turing machine model. The most frequently occurring transition rule determining changes between states would seem to be strongly analogous to material implication in formal logic. For example, the Turing machine quadruple, "$q1s0s1q2$," could be read, with its interpretation preserved, as material implication in formal logic, as "$(q1 \wedge s0) \rightarrow (s1 \wedge q2)$." It is perhaps unfortunate the Turing machine model should implicitly recall the logical connective that has been, both historically and in contemporary practice, simultaneously the most vexed and the most productive of the logical connectives. Material implication can be read as "If . . . then," except that difficulties in interpretation have tended to follow (Quine 1953: 84), particularly if a causal relation between antecedent and consequent is assumed. Similarly the state transition rule for Turing machines can be read as "If . . . then" (Johnson-Laird 1993: 161-162), but, unless this is deliberately restricted to an informal reading, comparable difficulties in interpretation are liable to follow. At the same time, the resemblance to the most productive logical connective may also partly account for the intuitive plausibility attached to the Turing machine model.

The overprinting of symbols is reminiscent of the formalist account of the computational process, and it is plausibly derived from, or at least influenced, by it. For mathematical formalism, it should be recalled, the process of computation was regarded as consisting of the writing, erasure, and substitution of symbols, according to given rules (Ramsey 1926a: 164-166). The replacement, in Turing machine computations, of one symbol by another from the given alphabet also recalls Wittgenstein's remark that "The method by which mathematics arrives at its equations is the method of substitution" (Wittgenstein 1922: 171).

These implicit connections to formal logic do hint at the possibility that the Turing machine model, rather than being received solely as an absolute account of the computational process, can also be read as an alternative formulation for formal logic. A remark from the *Tractatus Logico-Philosophicus* may again be relevant: "A particular method of symbolizing may be unimportant, but it is always important that this is a possible method of symbolizing" (Wittgenstein 1922: 59). From this perspective, the Turing machine model could be regarded as analogous to the primitive formulations of formal logic.

Logic

In contrast to the relative thematic unity of automata theory, formal logic is less unified in both its historical development and modern practice. One history of formal logic opens with the remark that "apart from 'philosophy' there is perhaps no name of a branch of knowledge that has been given so many meanings as 'logic'" (Bochenski 1961: 2). A continuity of analytic temperament, and a reluctance to trust to intuition, is admitted. Traces of such a temperament, insistent on consistency and intolerant of ambiguity, can be discerned in the tendency for logicians to obscure the diversity of logic and to present interpretations as if they were agreed accounts of a monolithic field.

Modern logic tends to be distinguished from previous logic by its more extensive use of notational symbols and mathematical methods. It has no sharp boundary that can be used to demarcate it from mathematics and, in contrast to the apparently intuitive plausibility of the Turing machine model, can be forbiddingly technical in character.

The notation of modern symbolic logic is also complex and varied. Modern logic, then, is not cohesive in either its themes or notation. Automata theory tended to draw on mathematical logic, for instance, when formalizing the Turing machine model, and to give examples of computational processes derived from mathematical domains.

A degree of consensus in modern logic is discernible with regard to the logical operators, although their application has changed historically, even since Boole (Boole 1854). It would seem to be generally agreed that the logical operators ($\wedge$, v, ~, ->, <->) are sufficient for the development of formal logic. The logical operators seem to be commonly regarded as functionally complete in the sense that to add further operators could only yield statements logically equivalent to statements already expressible with the given operators. Precisely delimited senses are prescribed for their use in formal logic and with reference to automata, which are not necessarily coincident with the senses their verbal correlates (and, or, not, if . . . then, if, and only if . . . then) can obtain in ordinary written or spoken discourse.

It would also seem to be agreed that the logical operators can be derived from more concise primitive formulations. For Whitehead and Russell in the first edition of the *Principia Mathematica*, published in 1913, it was to some extent (although not entirely) arbitrary, which two logical operators were to be taken as primitive. "~" and "v" were treated as the primitive operators and "~p" and "p v q" are taken as primitive expressions (Whitehead and Russell 1913: 1-7). The *Tractatus Logico-Philosophicus*, published in 1922 and following developments in symbolic logic since the *Principia Mathematica*, implicitly appeals to the concise expression, "~p $\wedge$ ~q" (Wittgenstein 1922: 15). It also offers a more satisfying account of the status of such concise formulations and asserts that "the proper general primitive signs are not *"p v q"*, *"(∃x).fx"*, etc., but the most general form of their combinations." (Wittgenstein 1922: 125-127). In the introduction to the second edition of the *Principia Mathematica* (published in 1925) "p|q", to be read as "~p v ~q", is introduced as the primitive idea (Whitehead and Russell 1913: 16). Other primitive formulations have been proposed (Bochenski 1961: 411-412).

Disagreement is marked upon the legitimate scope of a symbolic logic. One strong Anglo-American philosophical tradition has been to insist that ordinary discourse can be and, for analytical purposes, should be reduced to symbolic logic. For instance, in the *Principia Mathematica*, no distinction is made between contradictions expressible in the logical symbolism, such as the famous paradox connected with the class of all classes that are not members of themselves, and those that arise solely in connection with the discourse about that symbolism (Whitehead and Russell 1913). Subsequently, a distinction was made between logical and semantic contradictions in the *Principia Mathematica* (Ramsey 1926a). The distinction was later rephrased as a distinction between the object-language of a symbolic logic and the metalanguage of discourse about that logic. It has been widely, although not universally, accepted by those working in the analytic tradition developed by Russell (Kneale and Kneale 1962: 664).

More radical limitations of the useful scope of formal logic were indicated by F. P. Ramsey, who drew an incisive distinction between logic as a symbolic system and logic as the analysis of thought. In a critique of the *Principia Mathematica*, Ramsey stated:

> These two meanings of 'logic' are frequently confused. It really should be clear that those who say mathematics is logic are not meaning by 'logic' at all the same thing as those who define logic as the analysis and criticism of thought.

(Ramsey 1926a: 184)

This distinction was subsequently developed further. Formal logic was concerned "simply to ensure that our beliefs are not self-contradictory." In non-mathematical and non-scientific domains, it was not even clear that consistency was always beneficial: "human logic or the logic of truth is not merely independent of but sometimes actually incompatible with formal logic." The dominant philosophical tradition was acknowledged: "In spite of this nearly all philosophical thought about human logic and especially induction has tried to reduce it in some way to formal logic" (Ramsey 1926b: 87-88).

Object Language

Even given the significance of the distinction of human from formal logic, it is important to indicate the account of the object language endorsed. An account that is, in some sense, congruent with the consensus of automata theory and that would help make explicit the analogies already indicated between automata theory and formal logic would seem to have strategic value in encouraging their integration. For Gödel, and for subsequent commentators, the Turing machine model provided an absolute account of the computational process, whereas definitions in formal logic were inescapably linguistically relative.

An interpretation of formal logic analogous to the consensus of automata theory does exist, developed in the 1920s, prior to the formalization of the computational process, and apparently not yet integrated with Turing machine theory. For Wittgenstein in the *Tractatus Logico-Philosophicus* (Wittgenstein 1922), if we begin with truth-functions of atomic formulae, then to whatever extent we generalize upon them, we never reach propositions significantly different from those atomic truth functions. This interpretation of formal logic is congruent with the consensus of automata theory that modifications to the Turing machine model do not enlarge its computational power. The account of formal logic that can be derived from the *Tractatus Logico-Philosophicus* was subsequently explicated and extended to mathematics by Ramsey, particularly in "The foundations of mathematics" (Ramsey 1926a).

On this interpretation of the object language, and in brief, the predicate calculus is collapsed into the propositional calculus. The universal quantifier is treated as a conjunction whose writing cannot be completed and the existential quantifier as an uncompleted disjunction. For instance, (x).fx would be regarded as equivalent to $(fx_1 \wedge fx_2 \wedge fx_3 \ldots fx_n)$ and $\exists x.fx$ as equivalent to $(fx_1 \vee fx_2 \vee fx_3 \ldots fx_n)$. The only difference, on this interpretation, between the propositional and predicate calculus is:

that, owing to our inability to write propositions of infinite length, which is logically a mere accident, (ϕ) . ϕa cannot, like p . q, be elementarily expressed, but must be expressed as the logical product of the set of which it is also a member.

(Ramsey 1926a: 204)

The indispensable notational advantages following from the introduction of the quantifiers for unwritten conjunctions and disjunctions are still conceded.

Integration of Logic and Automata Theory

Such an interpretation of formal logic could be rendered more persuasive, and an integrated account of formal logic and automata theory obtained, if the contrast made by Gödel between an absolute formulation and a relative definition could be dissolved. It can then be replaced by a recognition that both automata theory and formal logic are socially constructed and historically specific modes of discourse. The particular contrast between the diagrams used in automata theory and the notational forms developed in formal logic can then be transformed into a final arbitrary distinction along a continuum from iconic to scriptorial signs, with no absolute epistemological authority attached to either mode of representation. The intention, then, is to preserve the forms of automata theory and of formal logic while reconciling their interpretation.

Gödel's comments on the absolute nature of Turing's model of the computational process can be read to recall themes inherited from Aristotle and Plato. For Plato, knowledge was founded on recollection of the ideal forms of ideas that existed prior to being known (Plato 385 BC: 130-154). Analogously, the model for the computational process is not regarded as a historically specific and humanly made construction, but as the discovery of an absolute idea. Aristotle regarded the perceptible as existing prior to perception, and as unaltered by the act of perception (Aristotle 323 BC: 21 and 43). A diagram, then, as a sensible, visual object can be granted absolute status. Yet the notion of absolute perception of ideal forms, existing independently of their knowers, has been increasingly questioned in the philosophy of science, the sociology of knowledge, and semiotics.

The distinction between an absolute definition and one tied to a particular formalism has been questioned in the philosophy of science. Kuhn in *The Structure of Scientific Revolutions* began to "suspect that something like a paradigm is prerequisite to perception itself." Aristotle and Galileo looked at swinging stones, and the first saw constrained fall, the second a pendulum: "The alternative is not some hypothetical 'fixed' vision, but vision through another paradigm, one which makes the swinging stone something else" (Kuhn 1970: 113-128). Fleck in *Genesis and Development of a Scientific Fact*, alluding to the curious nature of diagrams, poised between the evidently conventional system of writing and the seemingly more natural iconicity of aspects of the pictorial, asserted: "There is no visual perception except by ideovision and there is no other kind of illustration than ideograms" (Fleck 1979: 141). With regard to mathematical and logical constructions, concern must be focused on perception by social subjects, not personal or biological individuals. The same personal and biological individuals have been members of the intersecting discursive communities concerned with automata theory and formal logic. The absence of a fully integrated account would seem to testify to Fleck's observation that "the stylized uniformity of his [an individual's] thinking as a social phenomenon is far more powerful than the logical construction of his thinking" (Fleck 1979: 110). Acceptance of a dichotomy between an absolute formulation and a relative definition may also have been a factor inhibiting the development of a unified account. Yet, if the notion of innocent perception is rejected, this dichotomy can no longer be sustained.

The illusory nature of absolute perception and the intersubjective construction of reality have also been emphasized in the sociology of knowledge. For Berger and Luckmann in *The Social Construction of Reality*, reality was socially constructed and mediated. Spoken and written language, and other sign systems, were intersubjective experience rendered objective. Symbolic universes, broadly corresponding to the idea of a paradigm or thought community, were social products with a history. To understand their meaning, one had to understand the history of their production. Such symbolic universes did not have significant existence unless they were sustained by the beliefs of the agents involved in their construction and reproduction (Berger and Luckmann 1985: 85-142). Even if symbolic worlds are perceived in reified terms, they remain humanly made artifacts. The emphasis on the intersubjective construction of symbolic universes contrasts with the Platonic idea of recollection of ideal forms existing before being known, and not influenced by the act of knowing, and the Aristotelian emphasis on the perceptible existing apart from the act of perception.

Semiotics offers a way of recasting and refining the distinction made by Gödel between an absolute formulation and a relative definition into a contrast between types of sign. In some, although not all, semiotics, as for Fleck and Kuhn in the philosophy of science, it has become increasingly difficult to conceive of innocent perception without semiotic mediation, of signifieds existing independently of a sign system. The sign-system through which perception is mediated need not be purely verbal or reducible, without loss of distinctions, to verbal language. The diagram has already emerged as a curious graphic form, mixing, and often combining, iconic and notational elements. A specifically semiotic distinction of scriptorial from iconic signs (embodied in the contrast between the representations in Figure 1 (scriptorial) and Figure 2 (iconic)) can be used first to isolate the contrast between automata theory and formal logic and then to integrate the two discursive activities by suggesting that the distinction is better understood as a contrast along a continuum between types of sign, not as a dichotomy between a natural process and a deliberately constructed formalism.

The powerful analytical terminology for the study of signs developed by semiotics, and introduced into information science, can be recalled from Warner (Warner 1990). Aspects of the sign are differentiated. A sign is constituted by something standing for something else, by a relation between the thing signifying and the thing signified. Signifier, sign, and signified are typically distinguished. Form and meaning, expression and content convey a distinction similar, although not identical, to that of signifier from signified. The trichotomy of signifier, sign, and signified can yield a more sophisticated, incisive, and discriminating way of enforcing differentiations between aspects of the sign than can be obtained from any other known source. Representation in graphic form may help to clarify the relation between signifier, sign, and signified:

$$\text{signifier} \quad \rightarrow \quad \text{signified}$$
$$\text{sign}$$

The signifier lies at the beginning of an act of signification. It is linked to signified by a human subject, excluding, with the aim of analytical clarity, animal signification, or zoosemiosis. The sign is formed by the act of uniting a signifier to a signified. Expression, relation, and content can be shown in similar graphic form to signifier, sign, and signified:

$$\text{expression} \quad \rightarrow \quad \text{content}$$
$$\text{relation}$$

An expression is connected to a content, with the relation between expression and content existing in the interpreter's mind while that connection is being made (Warner 1990).

Different types of sign are also distinguished by semiotics. For instance, an index is indirect evidence of object or event signified, with a causal relation to that object or event, such as the footprint found by Robinson Crusoe or wet ground after rain or dew. For an icon, there is a resemblance between signifier and signified: Durer's drawing of a rhinoceros is given as one example of an iconic sign. Graphic signs can be distinguished from phonic signs. Within the graphic, scriptorial signs, exemplified by alphabetic written language, can be contrasted with pictorial signs. Texts differ in the number and types of sign distinguished, with a degree of arbitrariness in choice in distinctions made, and in interpretations given to terms for types of sign. Changes in the meaning of one term will tend to affect the senses taken by other terms in the cluster (Warner 1990).

The distinction between iconic and scriptorial signs can be expanded. Both are constituted by a contractual, not natural, relation between a signifying and signified aspect. For an icon, there is a resemblance between signifier and signified: the signifier is motivated by the signified. In contrast, for scriptorial signs, the connection between signifier and signified is arbitrary or unmotivated. The word "ox" has only an arbitrary relation to the mental image signified. Scriptorial signs, particularly written language, are often closely associated with speech, whereas iconic signs may not be given verbal or oral correlates. Yet, although this contrast may be one historical source for a harsh distinction of the scriptorial from the iconic, it will only partially serve to discriminate them. Rather, they can be discriminated along a continuum within the graphic, from motivated or analogical to an arbitrary or unmotivated connection between signifier and signified (Warner 1994: 9-44).

Conclusion

The particular contrast between an absolute or natural formulation and a relative definition can, then, be dissolved. It could be recast as a contrast along a continuum from iconic to notational. The elements of motivation in the Turing machine model may be one source for it being accepted as natural. The notion of the autonomous existence of proofs, not vivified by the beliefs of a thought community, can also no longer be accepted. The Turing machine model can now be regarded as a mathematical construction, with a specific historical origin. The distinction between the apparently absolute model of the computational process associated with the Turing machine formulation and the more clearly conventional models of formal logic has been recast as a more satisfactory distinction between predominantly iconic and notational forms. An account of formal logic congruent with the consensus of Turing machine theory has thereby been rendered more persuasive.

Why should the distinction between iconic and notational forms be a more satisfying formulation of the contrast and connections between automata theory and formal logic? It does not appeal to absolute definitions and regards both discursive activities as socially and historically situated. In contemporary terms, interest in computational operations has spread beyond the specialized research communities from which automata theory, formal logic, and working computers emerged. Other discursive communities have different and, arguably, equally valid criteria for discussion and proof. The Turing machine model could retain its strategic value as a common referent point for those interested in computational operations, although it need no longer be credited with absolute epistemological status. Each particular graphic formulation may be favored by particular discursive communities, and be given meaning by the beliefs of those communities, but no privileged, atemporal and asocial, epistemological

Chapter 5

Writing and Literary Work in Copyright: A Binational and Historical Analysis

Introduction

Copyright in the United Kingdom and the United States would seem to offer a delicate register from which to read changes in socially shared and endorsed concepts associated with communication and information. The texts in which such developments are embodied are, to varying extents, public in nature. Legislation has been sanctioned by elected representatives and judicial decisions can legitimately be regarded as attempts at consensual interpretation on behalf of a political community of statutes and previous cases. Even commentaries, prepared by individuals in more private capacities, tend to aim at similar interpretative ends to judgments. Such texts would seem to be appropriate subjects of study for the discipline of social epistemology envisaged by Shera in 1952 (Shera 1952). The focus of social epistemology was to be "upon the production, flow, integration and consumption of all forms of communicated thought throughout the entire social pattern" (Shera 1961: 16). Social epistemology was to be distinguished from existing forms of epistemology by its concern with the intellectual processes of "society *as a whole,*" rather than primarily of the individual (Shera 1952: 27). Within information science, at least, social epistemology remains a largely undeveloped discipline.

For Shera, social epistemology was also a potential source for a "kind of 'acculturation of the machine,'" of the computer (Shera 1961:

16). From the perspective of social epistemology, the incorporation of computer programs to copyright protection, together with other written products of intellectual labor, in U.K. and U.S. copyright law can be interpreted as a significant assimilation, rather than dismissed as a quaint labeling. In contrast, the U.K. *Data Protection Act 1984* gave British subjects some rights of access to computer-held information on themselves, but not to paper records. Commenting on this unhappy contrast in rights of access to information in the 1985 Panizzi lectures, D. F. McKenzie suggested that "one might feel that some central, unifying concept of 'the text' had broken down." Panizzi himself would have been disturbed at this loss of unity and "would have asked on what unifying, intellectual principle, does it [computing] relate to books?" (McKenzie 1986: 42-43). The treatment of documentary and computer-held information in recent U.K. legislation would seem to suggest complex and contradictory public attitudes to computers and books. In the context of copyright, computer programs have been assimilated to a category that already included documents, while computer-held and documentary information are awkwardly distinguished for the purposes of data protection.

Earlier developments in information technology, such as stenography and phonography, have been progressively, although not always smoothly or rapidly, incorporated into U.K. and U.S. copyright protection. Concomitant changes have tended to occur in the interpretation of significant terms connected with copyright. For instance, in the United Kingdom, the interpretations for writing and for a literary work, or other artifact in which copyright can subsist, have been extensively developed in copyright law since the *Copyright Act 1842*. Analogous, although not precisely parallel, developments have occurred in U.S. copyright. The constitutional term *writings*, for an artifact in which intellectual property can inhere, has been liberally interpreted since the 1870s in both statutes and significant cases. In both jurisdictions, an initial reluctance to admit new media to copyright protection tends to give way over time to the assimilation of such works.

The particular concepts associated with copyright whose development I wish to examine are, then, for the United Kingdom: those of writing, with some indications of distinctions made between written language and speech, and of a literary work or other artifact in which copyright can inhere, with special attention to the period from the *Copyright Act 1842*. Comparable, although not identical, developments occur in U.S. copyright law and I wish to trace the development of the interpretations assigned to writing, and to writings as artifacts in which copyright can inhere, over a broadly similar period.

It might be possible naively to assume that the United Kingdom and the United States would exhibit closely comparable histories with regard to the development of significant aspects of copyright. In addition to broader cultural and linguistic similarities, there are specific commonalities in the development of copyright: for instance, the first U.S. *Copyright Act of 1790* was strongly influenced by the U.K. *Copyright Act 1709*. Despite these commonalities, there are divergent patterns between the two jurisdictions with some evidence of convergence over time, particularly from the early twentieth century. Yet even during the 1970s, the deliberations of legislators do not seem to have been fully informed by a comparative perspective. For instance, computer programs were generally, although not necessarily universally, regarded as literary works for the purposes of copyright protection in the United Kingdom, prior to the confirmation of this categorization by legislation, whereas in the United States their status as artifacts for copyright was less clear and was established, not recognized, by legislation. However, legislators in the United States do not seem to have considered United Kingdom history or practice when formulating policy. A comparative study can, then, be valuable for exposing significant differences, as well as resemblances, between the two jurisdictions.

This exercise in social epistemology is undertaken with a dual intention. First, and most important, in connection with the challenge posed by McKenzie, to establish a unifying principle for documents and computers. Responses have already identified writing and the faculty for constructing socially shared systems of signs as such unifying principles (Warner 1994). Discovering comparable ideas in the public texts associated with copyright can lend a more consensual sanction to a development which remains marginal to information science. Second, retrospective analysis can lend a historical perspective to the assimilation of computer programs to copyright protection.

Copyright ca. 1842-1988

The guiding principle which has informed the extension of copyright protection since the early nineteenth century in both the United Kingdom and the United States has been that copyright should subsist in all works representing the product of a sufficient degree of intellectual skill or labor if so fixed that they can be reproduced (*Copyright and Designs Law* 1977: paragraph 28). The two aspects of this principle, the degree of intellectual labor and the amenability to reproduction, have tended to be used to discriminate those performances or artifacts admissible to copyright protection from those excluded. The principles informing the development of copyright have been simple; their application has been more complex and subject to dispute.

Technical innovations and social and political pressures can be discerned as influences on the development of copyright in both jurisdictions since the mid-nineteenth century. Forms of writing other than alphabetic written language, such as ciphers for telegraphic transmission and stenography for verbatim transcription, were increasingly developed in the nineteenth century and then impinged on copyright. Audio and audiovisual technologies, beginning with phonography, conferred the possibility of permanence on the sounds of utterance and other aspects of oral performances. Concern for copyright in computer programs emerged gradually after the development of the stored program computer in the 1940s and gathered strength during the 1970s (See chronology pp. 100-103).

The United Kingdom and the United States have distinctive, although partly parallel, histories. The United Kingdom was a signatory to the *Berne Convention of 1886* (*Berne Convention* 1886), and, thereafter, U.K. legislators have been concerned to bring domestic copyright into conformity with the most recent text of the convention. The *Universal Copyright Convention 1952* was also ratified by the United Kingdom. Concern for copyright in computer programs was not a factor in considerations for the *Copyright Act 1956*, but it is clearly causally connected with the terms of the *Copyright (Computer Software) Amendments Act 1985* and the *Copyright, Designs and Patents Act 1988*. Crucial developments, such as the admission of writing without meaning in ordinary language to copyright protection, begin to occur in cases heard in the 1880s and were later given statutory recognition in the *Copyright Act 1911* and the *Copyright Act 1956*.

The development of copyright in the United States shows similarities to the United Kingdom, with identifiable inheritances as well as significant differences. The U.S. Constitution gave "Authors . . . the exclusive Right to their . . . Writings" (*Constitution* 1789). The first U.S. *Copyright Act of 1790* was almost a verbatim copy of the *U.K. Act of 1710* (*Copyright Act* 1710; *Copyright Act* 1790). U.K. cases are cited as precedents in U.S. judgments, despite the differences following from a written constitution. Yet, the United States did not begin to grant protection to foreign authors until 1891 (*Copyright Act* 1891). Nor was it a signatory to the *Berne Convention of 1886*, although there are traces of its influence arising from the desire not to endanger rights granted to U.S. citizens in foreign countries. Significant developments, such as the denial that a musical roll infringed copyright inhering in a score and the extension of protection to ciphers for telegraphic transmission, occur in cases decided in the 1900s and 1920s. Their repercussions extend until after the *Copyright Act 1976*, when it was confirmed that computer programs would receive protection as literary works.

Writing

Similar issues arise in connection with the interpretation accorded to writing in U.K. and U.S. copyright at both comparable and markedly different dates, but judicial and legislative responses are different.

United Kingdom

The *Copyright Act 1842* was not explicitly concerned with the interpretation to be given to writing, although published documents were prominent among the categories of works accorded copyright protection (*Copyright Act* 1842). The interpretation assigned to writing was developed in U.K. copyright between 1884 and 1988, first by judicial decisions and in the interpretations placed upon them, and then by prescriptive definitions in legislation to include all forms of notation with equal status for the purposes of claims to copyright.

Three cases heard in 1884 and 1886 allowed copyright to subsist in contractions developed as part of a system of shorthand (Figure 1) and in ciphers compiled with the intention of enabling the elimination of errors in telegraphic transmissions. In *Pitman v. Hines*, the plaintiff was seeking to restrain publication of *One Thousand Contractual Outlines* on the grounds that it was substantially a copy from the "well-known system of phonography" developed by Pitman. The defendant claimed that "he had somewhat amplified the plaintiff's rules," but that copyright could inhere in contractions for shorthand was not contested. An injunction to restrain publication of *One Thousand Contractual Outlines* was granted as the defendant was considered to be "merely a copyist," rather than an independent author (*Pitman v. Hines* 1884: 3c). In *Ager v. Peninsular and Oriental Steam Company*, the plaintiff, Ager, had published *The Standard Telegram Code*, which consisted of some 100,000 words, selected from eight languages, and accompanied by numeric ciphers. Users of the work for the purposes of telegraphic transmission were to attribute meanings to the words or numeric ciphers and to communicate the significations they had chosen to their correspondents. The plaintiffs submitted that the defendants had copied from *The Standard Telegram Code*. The defendants denied copying, although, similarly, they did not contest that copyright could subsist in words not used for their usual meaning or in numeric ciphers. The plaintiff's case was upheld on the basis of the "usual test . . . [of] time and labour in compilation" (*Ager v. Peninsula* 1884: 642). The last of the three cases, *Ager v. Collingridge*, again concerned the infringement of copyright in the ciphers compiled by Ager. In this case, copyright was contested: "The defence was that the plaintiff's book was not a proper subject for copyright, that it did not contain any interpretation or equivalent in ordinary language of any of the telegraphic words comprised in it, so that every person was obliged before he could derive any benefit from it to attribute such of the telegraphic works as he desired to make use of some meaning or equivalent in ordinary language." The judgment recorded makes no explicit reply to this contention, but cited the earlier case involving Ager as an applicable precedent, and draws attention to the "infinite time and trouble" expended by Ager and his assistants in making the work. The report of the case in *The Times* concludes with: "His Lordship

14   CONSONANTS.

	Letter.	Phonograph.	Examples of its power.		Name.	Phonotype.
Explodents.	P	╲	ro*p*e	*p*ost	pee	p, *p*
	B	╲	ro*b*e	*b*oast	bee	b, *b*
	T	│	fa*t*e	*t*ip	tee	t, *t*
	D	│	fa*d*e	*d*ip	dee	d, *d*
	CH	╱	et*ch*	*ch*est	chay	ç, *ç*
	J	╱	ed*g*e	*j*est	jay	j, *j*
	K	──	lee*k*	*c*ane	kay	k, *k*
	G	──	lea*g*ue	*g*ain	gay	g, *g*
Continuents.	F	╲	sa*f*e	*f*at	ef	f, *f*
	V	╲	sa*v*e	*v*at	vee	v, *v*
	TH	(	wrea*th*	*th*igh	ith	ɉ, *ɵ*
	TH	(	wrea*th*e	*th*y	thee	ɖ, *ɖ*
	S	)	hi*ss*	*s*eal	ess	s, *s*
	Z	)	hi*s*	*z*eal	zee	z, *z*
	SH	╱	vi*ci*ous	*sh*e	ish	ʃ, *ʃ*
	ZH	╱	vi*s*ion	*	zhee	ʒ, *ʒ*
Nasals.	M	⌒	see*m*	*m*et	em	m, *m*
	N	⌣	see*n*	*n*et	en	n, *n*
	NG	⌣	si*ng*	*	ing	ŋ, *ŋ*
Liquids.	L	╱	fa*ll*	*l*ight	el	l, *l*
	R	╲ ╱	fo*r*	*r*ight	ar, ray	r, *r*
Coalescents.	W	⌐	*	*w*et	way	w, *w*
	Y	⌐	*	*y*et	yay	y, *y*
Aspirate.	H	╱ ϭ	*	*h*igh	aitch	h, *h*

Figure 1. Examples of Pitman's system of phonography. Source: I. Pitman. *A Manual of Phonography, Or, Writing by Sound: a Natural Method of Writing by Signs that Represent Spoken Sounds; Adapted to the English Language as a Complete System of Phonetic Shorthand.* London: Fred Pitman, Phonetic Depot; Bath: Isaac Pitman, Phonetic Institute, 1880, pp.14 and 57.

ADVANTAGES OF SHORTHAND.

(See Key, page 7.)

was clearly of the opinion that the plaintiff's work was a proper subject for copyright" (*Ager v. Collingridge* 1886: 3). Although the issue of whether copyright could subsist in contractions or ciphers was only raised in the last case, all three cases have been interpreted in subsequent commentaries as establishing that meaning in ordinary language, or "human readability" (Skone James et al. 1980: paragraphs 154-156), was not a requirement for copyright protection (Skone James 1948: 57; Skone James and Skone James 1965: paragraphs 153-154; Skone James et al. 1980: paragraphs 154-156; Niblett 1980: 44-45; Brett and Perry 1981; Dworkin 1984: 97; Philips 1986: 118).

Technologies for the mechanical reproduction of sounds began significantly to impinge on U.K. copyright in 1899. The plaintiffs in *Boosey v. Whight* held copyright in the music of three songs, "My lady's bower," "The better land," and "The Holy City." They "complained of the sale by the defendants of certain perforated sheets of paper for use in an instrument called the 'Aeolean' which externally resembled a cottage piano, but was really a wind instrument worked mechanically." The sheets of paper, or musical rolls, were interchangeable. The defendants conceded that the perforations could be transformed into musical notation with the aid of a key but still contested they were not intended to be read and did not appeal to human intelligence. The plaintiffs countered that the perforated sheets could be read, even if only with difficulty, and that their readability was "the true test of a notation of music being a sheet of music" under the terms of the *Copyright Act 1842*. The defendants contested that the legislature had never intended to deal with the mechanical reproduction of music, while the plaintiffs argued that barrel organs and similar instruments have never been sufficiently significant to be worth restraining. Neither plaintiffs nor defendants appealed to the previous cases involving ciphers and shorthand. The judgment held that a perforated roll was not a copy within the meaning of the Copyright Act, as it did not appeal to the eye, and was to be regarded as a "part[s] of a mechanical contrivance for producing musical notes" (*Boosey v. Whight* 1899: 574). The issue was not tested at the House of Lords and the judgment seems to have been regarded as unsatisfactory. It was deliberately overruled by the *Copyright Act 1911*, in accordance with the 1908 Berlin text of *Berne Convention* (*Berlin Convention* 1908). Copyright was to include the sole right to make a record, perforated roll, cinematograph film, or other contrivance by which a work might be mechanically performed or delivered. "Records, perforated rolls, and other contrivances by means of which sound may be mechanically reproduced" were to be regarded as musical works (*Copyright Act* 1911: § 19 (1)).

The *Copyright Act 1911* did not prescribe an interpretation of writing and seems to have been influenced, in respects which impinge on the treatment of writing, more by a desire to being U.K. legislation into conformity with the 1908 Berlin text of the *Berne Convention*, than by the cases involving ciphers and contractions for shorthand. Copyright protection continued to be accorded to published documents but as examples of the new legislative category of "original . . . literary work" (*Copyright Act* 1911). The Berlin text of the *Berne Convention* had defined literary or artistic works in which copyright could subsist to include "*any* production in the literary, scientific *or* artistic domain, whatever may be the mode or form of its *reproduction* . . . dramatic or dramatic-musical works, choreographic works and entertainments in dumb show, the acting form of which is fixed in writing or otherwise" (*Berlin Convention* 1908: Article 2). The *Copyright Act 1911* adopted a similar definition of a "dramatic work" as "any piece for recitation, choreographic work or entertainment in dumb show, the scenic arrangement of which is fixed in writing or otherwise" (*Copyright Act* 1911: § 35 (1)). An explicit requirement for fixation is made but the qualification "or otherwise" leaves it unclear whether the term *writing* covers forms other than written language, although were writing to be taken in its ordinary usage, it presumably would not. Judgments seem, then, to have preceded legislation in their admission of writing without meaning in ordinary language to copyright protection.

Difficulties in interpretation arising from potential anomalies between precedents judicially established and legislation are exemplified by a case heard in 1917, *D.P. Anderson & Co. v. The Lieber Code Company*. The plaintiffs had published the *Empire Cipher Code,* which consisted of some 100,000 five-letter sequences intended for the purposes of telegraphic transmission. They alleged that the defendants' publication, the *Lieber Code,* had unlawfully reproduced a substantial part of the *Empire Cipher Code.* The defendants contested copyright: the plaintiff's work is not an "original literary work" within the meaning of that expression in the *Copyright Act 1911* inasmuch as it is a mere compilation of unmeaning words arbitrarily constructed of five letters. Nothing can be "literary" which does not involve an appreciation of the meaning of words. In *Ager v. Peninsula and Oriental Steam Navigation Co.* and in *Ager v. Collingridge*, the code words in question were real words taken from different languages. J. Bailhache, presiding, is recorded as remarking: "What is the difference between making a code by taking a word from another language, but which is not used with the significance it bears in that language, and making a code out of artificially constructed words?" The defendants further denied that the Ager cases were any longer relevant due to differences between the 1842 and 1911 acts, drawing attention to the replacement of a book by an "original literary work" as an artifact in which copyright could subsist. In the earlier cases, the question was whether the work was a book within s.2 of the *Copyright Act 1842*, now the question is whether the plaintiff's code is an "'original literary work,' and it is submitted that it is not." The judgment held that the differences between the acts were not pertinent, cited the earlier cases involving the ciphers compiled by Ager as applicable precedents, and concluded that the plaintiffs were "right in saying that their code is a proper subject for copyright" (*Anderson v. Lieber* 1917: 421). This case has also been cited by subsequent commentators as establishing that writing need not have any meaning in ordinary language for the purposes of claims to copyright (Skone James 1948: 57; Skone James and Skone James 1965: paragraphs 153-154; Skone James et al. 1980: paragraphs 154-156; Niblett 1980: 44-45; Dworkin 1984: 97; Phillips 1986: 118).

Legislation and judicial precedent, and the interpretations placed upon them were reconciled with regard to writing by the *Copyright Act 1956*. Writing was to be interpreted as "any form of notation, whether by hand or by printing, typewriting or any similar process." The qualification "or otherwise" was omitted from the requirement for a dramatic work to be reduced to writing (*Copyright Act* 1956: § 48). The interpretation assigned to writing in the 1956 act was not positively influenced by the 1948 Brussels text of the *Berne Convention*, which retained the qualification "or otherwise" on the requirement for literary or artistic works to be reduced to writing (*Brussels Convention* 1948: Article 2) nor by the *Universal Copyright Convention 1952*, which did not prescribe interpretations of the works to be protected (*Universal Copyright Convention* 1952). Nor was it influenced by a concern with intellectual property in computer programs as the potential significance of this issue was not recognized at all in considerations for the Act (*Copyright and Designs* 1977: paragraph 479).

In contrast, concern with copyright in computer programs motivated the *Copyright (Computer Software) Act 1985* and was a significant consideration for the *Copyright, Patents and Designs Act 1988*. The few applications that had reached the courts prior to the 1985 act tended to claim copyright protection for programs as "original literary works" (Dworkin 1984: 96). The 1985 and 1988 acts explicitly extended protection to programs as "original . . . literary works" (*Copyright Act* 1985: § 1; *Copyright Act* 1988: § 3). The 1988 act refrained from defining a program with the intention of covering the widest possible range of technical developments (*Current Law* 1989). Writing is to be interpreted to include "any form of notation or code, whether by hand or otherwise and regardless of the method by which, or medium in or on which, it is recorded" (*Copyright Act* 1988: § 178). The clauses added to the interpretation prescribed in the 1956 Act, "or code" and "regardless of the method by which, or medium in or on which it is recorded," have been taken to confer a new scope (*Current Law* 1989). From a historical perspective, recognition of computer programs as literary works and the further development of the interpretation of writing are comprehensible as part of a pattern whereby existing categories have been expanded to accommodate technical developments.

The interpretation of writing was, then, developed in U.K. copyright, with discernible pressures from technical innovations, until meaning in ordinary language was explicitly not criterial to the recognition of writing. For the purposes of copyright, no special legal status is accorded to written language as distinguished from other forms of writing. These public developments are analogous to the later, still marginal, differentiation of written from spoken language and the recognition of forms of writing not necessarily linked to utterance within linguistics.

United States

Writing, in the sense of coded graphic inscription, is less sharply demarcated as a significant category in U.S. than U.K. copyright. It tends to be absorbed into "writings," the constitutional term for an artifact in which copyright could subsist. In contrast, in the United

Kingdom writing as a graphic form is distinguished from a book and then a literary work as artifacts for copyright. Similar technologies occur in copyright disputes, although at different dates and with contrasting judicial and legislative responses.

The legislative context for subsequent developments is partly provided by the 1865 amendment to the *Copyright Act 1831* and the *Copyright Act 1870*. The 1865 amendment introduced photographs and their negatives into the list of artifacts for copyright (*Copyright Act 1865*). The *Copyright Act 1870* further extended protection to "painting[s], drawing[s], chromo[s], statue[s], statuary, and . . . models or designs intended to be perfected as works of the fine arts" (*Copyright Act 1870*: § 86). From the 1870s onward, then, Congress began to give a liberal interpretation to the constitutional term "writings" (Holland 1978: 12; *Copyright Act 1882*).

A case, *White-Smith v. Apollo*, which was subsequently to become significant to the interpretations assigned to copying and to writing was considered by the Supreme Court in 1908. A musical roll had been produced without permission of the copyright holders of the original compositions and the plaintiffs sought to restrain the alleged infringement of copyright in "Little Cotton Dolly" and "Kentucky Babe Schottische." The action was refused. The judgment noted that in all comparable cases mechanical producers of musical tones had not been considered to be within the protection offered by the copyright act. Under the *Berne Convention of 1886* mechanical reproduction of music did not constitute infringement of copyright, and, although the United States was not a signatory to that agreement, it was politic to maintain parity in domestic practice in order to ensure that rights accorded to U.S. citizens in foreign countries would not be endangered. A copy of a musical composition was "a written or printed record of it in intelligible notation." It was "strained and artificial" to say that a mechanical instrument that reproduces a tune copies it (*White-Smith v. Apollo* 1908: 2984-2985). Statute did not provide for the protection of the intellectual conception apart from its tangible existence, whatever the value of that conception. If the liberal interpretation of copying contended for by the appellants were granted then other mechanical devices for the production of sounds, such as gramophone records, would be admitted to copyright protection. All these devices were well known when the various copyright acts were passed and had Congress intended to protect them it could have been explicit. The denial in the

U.K. case of *Boosey v. Whight* (1899) that a musical roll constituted an infringement on copyright in a score was cited as a precedent (*White-Smith v. Apollo* 1908).

Did the matrix of perforations constitute a writing, although this issue was subordinate to, and not easily distinguishable from, the question of copying? Musical rolls were not intended to be read by the eye, although there was "some testimony to the effect that great skill and patience might enable the operator to read his record as he could a piece of music written in staff notation" (*White-Smith v. Apollo* 1908: 2985). The absence of an intention to produce a visually intelligible notation, and the degree of labor and special knowledge involved in deciphering by visual inspection, seem to have debarred the matrix from being considered a writing.

A musical roll was not then a copy of a score, nor a writing in itself, for the purposes of copyright. Subsequent commentaries have interpreted this judgment as constituting an equation of the "intelligible" and the "visible" since the piano rolls would be intelligible to the ear (Nimmer 1990: 2.08 [A] n.8). Mr. Justice Holmes, while concurring with the denial of copying, commented that it gave to "copyright less scope than its rational significance and the ground on which it is granted seem to demand." If a work was to be protected at all, it should be protected according to its essence. If the statute was too narrow, the definition of copy should be expanded by statutes. Although he agreed with the judgment as an interpretation of existing law, he was dissatisfied with the law itself (*White-Smith v. Apollo* 1908: 2986).

The subsequent *Copyright Act 1909* deliberately amended the interpretation of copying established by the judgment in *White-Smith v. Apollo* (Abrams 1991: Section 2.04 [c] [3] [viii]), although mechanical contrivances for producing sounds were still not to be considered writings. Copyright in a musical composition included the right "to make any arrangement or setting of it or of the melody of it in any system of notation or any form of record in which the thought of an author may be recorded and from which it may be read or reproduced." Once a copyright proprietor had consented to the use of a copyrighted work "upon the parts of instruments serving to reproduce mechanically the musical work," any other person could make use of the work upon payment of a royalty to the copyright proprietor (*Copyright Act* 1909: § 1 (e)). Although it was now established that a musical roll could constitute a copy of a score, the musical roll itself, and comparable contrivances, were not to be regarded as writings.

The subtle distinction embodied in the 1909 act, between copying and a writing in itself, seems to have lent itself to ambiguous interpretation. The judgment in *White-Smith v. Apollo* became significant from frequent subsequent citation, although the artificial distinctions between different material forms that it embodied have been regretted. Protection for computer programs was felt to be uncertain following the judgment and under the 1909 Act. For instance, the object code of a program could be considered analogous to the matrix of perforations on a musical roll: it is not intended to be read by the eye, is visually decipherable only with extreme difficulty, and is capable of controlling the motions of a machine. A program could be copyrightable, presumably as source code, as a tangible expression of intellectual labor, but this need not prevent the unauthorized duplication of the object code. The *White-Smith v. Apollo* judgment, then, became significant for reasons not anticipated at the time. It also seems to have been uncritically cited, without necessarily referring to Mr. Justice Holmes' comments on the unsatisfactory state of the law or to the different interpretation of copying deliberately embodied in the 1909 Act. The judgment does not seem to have been considered to have been fully overruled until the 1980 amendment to copyright (Rose 1982).

A significant case, *Reiss v. National Quotation Bureau*, concerned with whether copyright could subsist in coined words compiled for cable correspondence, and thereby similar in subject to cases previously considered in the United Kingdom, was heard by the New York District Court in 1921. The only question raised was whether copyright could subsist in the *Simplix Pocket Blank Code*, which consisted of 6,325 words of 5 letters each. The words themselves had no meaning but were to be given an agreed meaning for the purposes of cable correspondence. The defendants denied that such coined words were the "writing" of an author. The judgment noted that the words, although they had no meaning, were susceptible of pronunciation. However, the ability to supply oral correlates does not seem to have influenced the extension of copyright protection. Instead, the judgment concentrated on the question of meaning. The coined words had only a prospective meaning, which they had not yet received, "like an empty pitcher." The distinction was admitted to be real, but, for all practical purposes irrelevant. Writing, without meaning, could be invented. Not all words communicate ideas: some are spontaneous ejaculations and some are used for their sound alone; there are meaningless rhymes, for instance the syllogistic mnemonic, "Barbara celarent"[1]. Music, presumably as a score, although this is not made explicit and there is no citation to *White-Smith v. Apollo*, is a writing, but does not normally have a representative meaning. If non-representative plastic arts are "writings," then such words could be, even though they communicate nothing. Words without meaning could still have aesthetic or practical uses, be the product of high ingenuity or even genius. There was no reason to limit the Constitution in any such way as the defendants required. Nothing in the American reports could be found that was remotely relevant, thereby implying that *White-Smith v. Apollo* (concerned with musical rolls) was not pertinent. The Ager cases were cited as precedents for granting protection to writing without meaning in ordinary language. Although these cases were heard in the United Kingdom under an act of Parliament not limited by any constitution, they were still relevant. The U.S. Constitution did not "embalm[s] inflexibly the habits of 1789 . . . its grants of power to Congress comprise, not only what was then know, but what the ingenuity of men should devise thereafter." The grant of the Constitution, here with regard to "writings," should be interpreted by "the general practices of civilized peoples in similar fields." The motion was denied and copyright in coined words without immediate meaning upheld (*Reiss v. National Quotation Bureau* 1921: 346-348). Subsequently, the judgment came to be regarded as a touchstone for a liberal interpretation of "writings" (*Goldstein v. California* 1973; CONTU 1978: 35-36). The issue of the admission to copyright protection of writing without meaning in ordinary language, which was to become significant in the United Kingdom, seems to have been less noticed. The application of the judgment to computer programs is unclear. It could be read as a precedent for the admission of source code to protection, although only more doubtfully of the object code. The object code would seem to be excluded, or at least of uncertain status by the *White-Smith v. Apollo* judgment, which denied copyright to musical rolls.

The status of computer programs in relation to copyright protection was, then, unresolved before the *Copyright Act 1976*. In three cases heard by the Supreme Court, computer programs had been denied patent protection, although this was not considered unambiguously to imply that they could not be patentable subject matter (CONTU 1978: 42). Computer programs have been considered as problematic an invention for patent law as they have been a writing for copyright law (U.S. Congress. Office of Technology Assessment 1986: 85). The status of writing without meaning in ordinary language or not amenable to visual interpretation without specialized skills is also unclear, with apparently relevant judicial precedents (concerned with musical rolls and ciphers) potentially subject to contradictory readings and subtle distinctions in legislation liable to ambiguous interpretation.

The *Copyright Act 1976* did not mention computer programs and commentaries differ in their interpretation of the extent of coverage offered. Copyright protection was to subsist in "original works of authorship fixed in any tangible medium of expression, now known or later developed, from which they can be perceived, reproduced, or otherwise communication, either directly or with the aid of a machine or device" (*Copyright Act*, 1976, § 102). The broad language concerning fixation has been interpreted as a deliberate avoidance of the artificial distinctions between media of expression derived from cases such as *White-Smith v. Apollo* (Miller 1981: 69). *Reiss v. National Quotation Bureau* (concerned with ciphers for telegraphic transmission) does not seem to have been considered relevant to the issue of the protection of computer programs, although cases concerned with comparable subjects have been significant to the interpretation assigned to writing in U.K. copyright. Commentators on the *Copyright Act 1976* have remarked that the law remained unclear with regard to the protection of computer programs (CONTU 1978: 28), although they have tended to interpret it as extending protection to them as "literary works" (Henderson 1983: 263; Rose 1982: 270). Literary works were works of authorship expressed in "words, numbers, or other verbal or numerical symbols or indicia regardless of the nature of the material objects, such as books, periodicals, manuscripts, phonorecords, film, tapes, disks, or cards, in which they are embodied" (*Copyright Act* 1976: § 101). Congress is also on record as considering that computer programs could be assimilated to protection without changes in statute (CONTU 1978: 37). The issue was still to be a matter for review and legislation.

CONTU, the National Commission on New Technological Uses of Copyrighted Works, which reported to Congress in 1978, recommended that computer programs should be incorporated into copyright protection. In accord with the tenor of their discussions, they have since been generally, although not necessarily exclusively, regarded as literary works, although this categorization does not seem to have been part of CONTU's formal recommendations (CONTU 1978), and, in contrast to the United Kingdom, the different categories for copyright protection are of little legal significance. Accordingly, the 1980 amendment to the copyright act added the term *computer program* to the list of defined expressions. A program was defined, rather restrictively, as "a set of statements or instructions to be used directly or indirectly in order to bring about a certain result" (*Copyright Act* 1980). Courts have subsequently given a liberal interpretation to this definition (*Apple v. Franklin* 1982). No explicit interpretation was assigned to writing, although the broad language concerning the requirement for fixation is comparable to the liberal interpretation assigned to writing in U.K. copyright statute (*Copyright Act* 1980).

In summary, comparable technologies impinged on the development of the interpretation accorded to writing in U.K. and U.S. copyright, although at different dates and with contrasting responses. Writing is more clearly demarcated as a significant category in U.K. than U.S. copyright. In the United Kingdom, writing is effectively made coextensive with all forms of notation. Later legislation in the United States could be interpreted as offering similar sanction to a concept of writing to include notations without meaning in ordinary language, for instance, in the requirement for fixation and definition of a literary work in the 1976 act. The status of computer programs with regard to copyright protection was also less clear in the United States prior to recent legislation (1976 and 1980), although they were explicitly incorporated by the 1980 amendment.

Speech

The principle that all works representing the fixed and reproducible product of intellectual labor should be accorded copyright protection has guided the protection granted to speech in both the United Kingdom and the United States. Technologies for conferring permanence on speech were developed or increasingly used from the mid-nineteenth century: first stenography, then phonography, and then other audio and audiovisual media. Works in such technologies have been assimilated to copyright protection, although there have been delays between the emergence of concern for intellectual property in such products and the extension, by judicial precedent or legislation, of copyright protection to them.

United Kingdom

Spoken performances not rendered permanent by reduction to writing or other material form have been treated differently from those which have been fixed. *Extempore* speech has never been protected (Phillips 1986: 4). Where spoken performances have been reduced to writing alone, copyright has usually been held to reside with the author of the written record. An *author* is difficult to define but *authorship* has usually been connected with intellectual, not predominantly physical, labor in transcription. For instance, under the 1842 act copyright was held to reside with the reporter of a public speech as stenography, under such circumstances, "involved skill and brainpower, beyond the mere mechanical operation of writing" (*Walter v. Lane* 1900: 555). In contrast, an amanuensis would seem not to acquire copyright by taking dictation (Phillips 1986: 115; Skone James and Skone James 1965: paragraph 153). Intellectual property in works in audio technologies, categorized as musical works, was accorded legislative recognition by the 1911 act, overruling the judicial precedent of *Boosey v. Whight*, but in conformity with the 1908 Berlin revision of the *Berne Convention* (*Berlin Convention* 1908). Sound recordings were introduced as a category in which copyright could subsist by the 1956 Act (*Copyright Act* 1956). The 1988 act continued to extend protection to sound recordings. In contrast, unrecorded speech, not reduced to writing, and therefore not amenable to replication, is not listed among the categories of work in which copyright can subsist and would therefore be excluded from protection (*Copyright Act* 1988). Although the development of copyright law in relation to spoken performances, as in other respects, is both complex and open to differing interpretations, principles of permanence and intellectual labor seem to have been consistently used to determine whether verbal performances are proper subjects for copyright.

Spoken and written language are then contrasted in U.K. copyright. The convergence of the communicative possibilities of recorded speech with those of written language, of transmission over space and time, has also been implicitly acknowledged by admitting it to protection, although under different conditions.

United States

Comparable, although not identical, patterns can be detected in U.S. copyright. Purely ephemeral performances, whether audio, visual, or audiovisual, such as a live television broadcast that is not recorded (U.S. House of Representatives 1976) are explicitly excluded from protection. *Extempore* speech would therefore not be covered. Protection of spoken words could only be claimed, under the guiding principles of copyright, when it is made permanent, either by transcription or recording, and embodies a sufficient degree of intellectual labor.

The law is complex, open to different interpretations, and not fully tested judicially with regard to unrecorded speech. In one case, *Jenkins v. News Syndicate 1926*, in which a newspaper editor had adapted a reporter's spoken version of a piece, without that reporter's consent, copyright was held to reside with the reporter. However, the reporter had reduced the spoken version to written notes (*Jenkins v. News Syndicate* 1926) and the judgment could only doubtfully be interpreted as establishing copyright in unrecorded speech.

The status of recorded speech in federal copyright has changed during the twentieth century. Following the *White-Smith v. Apollo* judgment (1908) and the *Copyright Act 1909*, mechanical devices for the reproduction of sounds, including spoken word recordings, were considered to be excluded from federal copyright protection. The interests of producers or authors of sound recordings could be and, in some instances, were protected by state, rather than federal, legislation. The constitutionality of state protection for sound recordings was established by *Goldstein v. California 1973*, in which the Supreme Court held that a California statute prohibiting unauthorized recordings, for sale, of published recordings was constitutional, as "writings" was to be "interpreted to include any physical rendering of fruits of creative and intellectual or aesthetic labor" (*Goldstein v. California* 1973: 247). Recordings fixed after February 12, 1972, were admitted to federal copyright protection by an amendment that came into force on that date (Miller 1981: 195). The 1976 act explicitly listed sound recordings as a category of work in which copyright could subsist (*Copyright Act* 1976).

Similar principles of permanence and intellectual labor, which guided the extension of copyright to the spoken word in the United Kingdom, seem to have been employed to discriminate verbal performances admissible to copyright protection from those excluded in the United States. An implicit contrast between the transitory nature of unrecorded speech and the permanence of writing, as well as an acknowledgement of the convergence of the communicative possibilities of recorded speech and written language, can similarly be read from the development of U.S. copyright.

Literary Work and Other Artifacts for Copyright

Both the United Kingdom and the United States have witnessed a progressive assimilation of new information technologies to copyright protection. Comparable, although also contrasting, developments have occurred in the categories of work distinguished for copyright protection.

United Kingdom

The category of an original literary work was introduced to U.K. copyright legislation by the 1911 act and replaced that of the book in the 1842 act as an artifact in which copyright could subsist. A literary work was to be interpreted as including "maps, charts, plans, tables, and compilations" (*Copyright Act* 1911: § 35 (1)). The 1956 act retained the term, original literary work, but assigned a more restricted interpretation: a literary work was to "include any written table or compilation" (*Copyright Act* 1956: § 48 (1)). The documentary forms having been omitted, maps, charts, and plans were to be protected as drawings within the category of artistic works. Such enumerative guides to interpretation do not make any explicit exclusions and they have not been regarded as exhaustive. Judgments and commentaries have conceded that a literary work may be intuitively easier to recognize than to define (Skone James and Skone James 1965: paragraph 152; Phillips 1986: 119).

Writing, in the sense developed with U.K. copyright of any form of notation, has been necessary, although never sufficient, to constitute a literary work. There must also be a degree of intellectual skill or labor in construction (Phillips 1986: 118). For instance, titles of works are not in themselves entitled to copyright protection, unless they are so long or complicated as to show skill or labor in their making. In contrast, the work involved in constructing catalogues, directories, and other lists of items in themselves embodying insufficient skill or labor for copyright protection has been judged to render such compilations proper subjects for copyright (Flint 1985: 12-33).

The 1911 act extended copyright protection to original literary, artistic, or musical works. Subsequent developments in information-carrying media have been assimilated to copyright protection. For instance, the 1956 act gave legislative sanction to copyright subsisting in cinematograph films and television and sound broadcasts, as Part II works, governed by different conditions from the literary, dramatic, or musical works of Part I (*Copyright Act* 1956). The 1988 act continued to extend protection to original literary, dramatic, or musical works, as well as sound recordings (*Copyright Act* 1988). Commentaries suggest that such categories are intended to be exhaustive, but that each category is open to liberal interpretation and to the incorporation of new types of work. Assimilation of innovations and developments to copyright protection has been guided by the reiterated principle that copyright should subsist in "almost all works representing the product of labour and/or skill, if fixed so that they can be reproduced" (*Copyright and Designs* 1977: paragraph 28). The principles informing the development of an artifact in which copyright can inhere have remained constant since 1842, and are still simple; the categories for such artifacts seem to have become increasingly complex and difficult to understand.

United States

The Constitution of the United States gave "Authors . . . the exclusive Right to their . . . Writings" (*U.S. Constitution* 1789). It may have been influenced by the contemporary idea of the natural rights of the author as a creative individual (Ringer 1974: 26), although it is difficult to reconstruct constitutional intentions in this respect.

The *Copyright Act 1790*, itself heavily indebted to the United Kingdom *Copyright Act 1710*, granted "author and authors of any map, chart, book or books . . . the sole right and liberty of printing, reprinting, publishing and vending such map, chart, book or books" (*Copyright Act* 1790). *Writings* in the Constitution has been given a broad and dynamic meaning, and innovations in information technologies have been progressively assimilated to protection. From the 1870s onward, Congress began to give a broad interpretation to writings (*Copyright Act* 1870; *Copyright Act* 1882; Holland 1978: 8-12). The judgment in *Reiss v. National Quotation Bureau* (1921), that the grant of the Constitution to Congress was that copyright should "comprise, not only what was then known, but what the ingenuity of men should devise thereafter," has been regarded as a touchstone for a liberal interpretation of writings (CONTU 1978: 35). The judgment of the Supreme Court in *Goldstein v. California* in 1973, that a writing included "any physical rendering of the fruits of creative intellectual or aesthetic labor," could be regarded as a confirmation and extension of a liberal interpretation (*Goldstein v. California* 1973; CONTU 1978: 110-111). Protection has never been withdrawn from a type of work admitted to copyright protection (CONTU, 1978: 37). The *Copyright Act 1976* replaced the constitutional term *writings* by "original works of authorship" as the embracing category for an artifact for copyright (*Copyright Act* 1976: § 102). Various subcategories of works of authorship were distinguished, from literary works to sound recordings, although the enumeration was not designed to be exhaustive. Congress's intention was neither to freeze the scope of copyrightable matter nor to allow unlimited expansion into areas completely outside present congressional intent (U.S. House of Representatives 1976). A progressive, although not entirely smooth, incorporation of works in new information technologies to copyright protection can be discerned in the period ca. 1860-1980, together with increasing complexity in legislation, judicial precedent, and categories for copyright protection.

Comparable developments, then, occurred in U.S. and U.K. copyright, with the progressive incorporation of new forms and a consequential increase in the complexity of the law. Terminological contrasts seem to have enabled, and discouraged, the growth of substantive distinctions. In particular, in the United Kingdom writing is both terminologically and substantively distinguished from a book or literary work. In contrast, the United States term *writings* of an author, which was sustained until the 1976 act, does not easily allow a comparable terminological contrast and, plausibly, may have discouraged the development of a substantive distinction, despite the significance attached to the *Reiss v. National Quotation Bureau* judgment concerned with ciphers for cable correspondence.

Conclusion

From a historical perspective, the categorization of computer programs as literary works by the 1985 and 1988 acts in the United Kingdom can be understood as a continuation of the established trend to incorporate developments in information-carrying media to copyright protection. The categories to which developments are assimilated are themselves modified in the process. In particular, since the 1880s, writing has been developed to include all forms of notation and the interpretation assigned to a literary work or other artifact in which copyright could inhere progressively expanded to encompass innovations in information-carrying media.

A similar incorporation of computer programs to copyright protection was made in the United States by the amendment of 1980. The path to this assimilation was less smooth and the amendment established, or at least greatly clarified rather than recognized, the status of programs as artifacts for copyright. From the 1870s onward, Congress began to give a liberal interpretation to the constitutional term *writings*. Yet the denial in the *White-Smith v. Apollo* judgment of 1908 that the production of a musical roll constituted infringement of copyright in a musical work was taken to imply that reproduction of a computer program would not constitute an infringement on the source code, despite the different interpretation assigned to copying in the *Copyright Act 1909*. The precedent established by the *White-Smith v. Apollo* judgment does not seem to have been considered to be fully overruled until the 1980 amendment. The admission of ciphers compiled for cable transmission to protection and, even more, the definition of literary works in the 1976 act could be taken as equating writing with all forms of notation, but this would be an imposed interpretation, rather than a reading legitimated by explicit guides to interpretation. In both jurisdictions, purely transitory speech has never been admitted to protection.

A comparative reading of the development of copyright in the United Kingdom and the United States suggests that the United States inherited some patterns from the United Kingdom; that chance events can significantly affect the development of the law by judicial precedent; and that, partly as a consequence of such events, copyright law in the United Kingdom and United States diverged. A convergence of practices is now evident. For instance, the United States derived its first copyright statute from the United Kingdom *Copyright Act 1710* and cases heard in the United Kingdom are cited as applicable precedents in U.S. judgments. Yet cases concerned with similar subjects, such as the extension of protection to ciphers, occur at markedly different dates, apparently largely by chance rather than deliberate policy, and are subject to different interpretations. Increasing similarities in practices between the two jurisdictions are now detectable. In 1921, the judgment in *Reiss v. National Quotation Bureau* recommended that the grant of the Constitution should be interpreted by "the general practices of civilized peoples in similar fields" (*Reiss v. National Quotation Bureau* 1921). Increasing transnational exchange of information seems to have enforced further convergence, even where jurisdictions are not common signatories of an international agreement. Most obviously concern for copyright in computer programs began to gather strength in the 1970s, some time after the development of the stored program computer in 1944, and programs are now regarded as artifacts for copyright in both jurisdictions.

The public texts associated with the development of copyright in the United Kingdom and the United States do provide a more consensual analogue to the single faculty for constructing socially shared systems of signs, and the recognition of forms of writing independent of speech, which have been identified as uniting and differentiating documents and computers. The principle informing the development of copyright in both jurisdictions, namely, that works representing the product of intellectual skill or labor, if so fixed that they can be reproduced, invokes a capacity analogous to, although differently stated from, the semiotic faculty (Warner 1994). With discernible influence from technical innovations and developments from the 1880s onward, the interpretation of writing for U.K. copyright was adapted to include, with equal status, all forms of notation, whether or not they had meaning in ordinary language. Written artifacts without meaning in ordinary language, other than computer programs, have been admitted to copyright protection in the United States, although judgments and commentaries do not seem to have cited this as a precedent for equating writing and notation. Significant forms that could be regarded as writing, such as the matrix of marks on a musical roll, have also been denied protection by both the judiciary and legislature. The development of U.S. copyright offers only qualified sanction for a liberal interpretation of writing. In both nations, a contrast between the permanence of written language and evanescence of unrecorded speech has also been given implicit judicial and legislative recognition, by not admitting purely transitory performances to protection. The permanence granted to spoken performances by developments in audio and audiovisual media has been implicitly acknowledged by the extension of copyright protection to them, although at a significantly later date in U.S. statute. Changes in the scope of categories for copyright protection occur first prior to, and apparently still independently of, the recognition of a single faculty for constructing systems of signs and of writing not linked to speech as developed in linguistics and semiotics.

In contrast to such painfully wrought and deliberately explicit development, the growth of analogous concepts in U.K. and U.S. copyright tends to be only implied or simultaneously qualified. The collocation made by both legislatures by subsuming documents in ordinary written language and computer programs within the category of literary work can be read to imply, but does not state, that they are mutually connected by the presence of writing and as the product of intellectual labor. In the United Kingdom, committees convened to review copyright have repeatedly expressed concern over difficulties in interpretation arising from the unusual meanings acquired by such terms as literary work (*Copyright and Designs* 1977: paragraph 17). Members of U.S. commissions have also considered that copyright terms such as authors, writings, and literary works have been stretched too far beyond the meanings they could obtain in ordinary discourse (CONTU 1978: 67-75). These reservations suggest that even explicitly assigned interpretations, such as those prescribed for writing in the United Kingdom 1956 and 1988 acts and the classification of computer programs as literary works, do not indicate that legislators have unreservedly endorsed the concepts to which they have given public sanction. The terminology of copyright and of ordinary discourse seems to amount to different languages, with uncertain and mutable boundaries intermingled in the minds of legislators and the texts they produce.

Concepts held within one language can conflict with those held in another. Such socially shared languages can disguise contradictions from individual consciousness. Thought itself seems to be conducted, at least in part, in socially shared systems of signs (Fleck 1979; Volosinov 1929). The social nature of thought provides a central justification for the focus of social epistemology on social rather than primarily individual ways of knowing: that knowledge is acquired, reformed, and disseminated by individuals living within social contexts which inescapably influence, although they do not necessarily determine, their thought.

Chronology of significant information technology developments, United Kingdom and United States copyright cases and legislation, and international conventions (dates for information technology developments are approximations)

Date	Information technology development	United Kingdom case	United Kingdom legislation
1710			*Copyright Act (1709)*
1789			
1790			
1831			
1842			*Copyright Act (1842)*
1854	Sounder telegraph		
1865			
1867			
1870			
1876	Phonograph		
1882			
1884		*Pitman v. Hines* *Ager v. Peninsula*	
1886		*Ager v. Collingridge*	
1891			
1895	Cinematograph		
1899		*Boosey v. Whight*	
1901	Radio		
1908			
1909			
1911			*Copyright Act (1911)*
1917		*Anderson v. Lieber*	
1921			
1926	Television Sound films		
1928			

Chronology *continued*

United States Case	United States legislation	International convention
	Constitutional provision concerning copyright *Copyright Act 1790* *Copyright Act 1831*	
	1865 Amendment *1867 Amendment* *Copyright Act 1870*	
	1882 Amendment	
		Berne Convention (1886)
	1891 Amendment	
White-Smith v. Apollo		*Berlin Convention (1908)*
	Copyright Act (1909)	
Reiss v. National Quotation Bureau		
		Rome Convention (1928)

Chronology *continued*

Date	Information technology development	United Kingdom case	United Kingdom legislation
1944	Programmable computer		
1948			
1952			
1956			*Copyright Act 1956*
1971			
1973			
1976			
1980			
1982			
1985			*Copyright (Computer Software) Amendment Act (1985)*
1988			*Copyright, Designs and Patents Act (1988)*

Chronology *continued*

United States Case	United States legislation	International convention
		Brussels Convention (1948) *Universal Copyright Convention (1952)*
		Paris Convention (1971)
Goldstein v. California		
	Copyright Act (1976) *1980 Amendment*	
Apple v. Franklin		
		Berne Convention Implementation Act 1988

Chapter 6

Is There an Origin to Graphic Communication?

Introduction

The idea of a transition to an information society, emblematized by the computer, has tended to be conceived as a radical disjunction, a "turning point[s] in modern history" (Bell 1980: 509, 544). There are traces of technological determinism in the stress on the autonomous significance of the computer. In other discussions, the computer itself is characterized as a "radical novelty" (Dijkstra 1989), implicitly viewed in isolation from other preexisting and continuing information technologies.

The idea of an abrupt disjunction in the transition to an information society, and the associated view of the computer as a radical novelty, can be tempered by a perspective that insists that information technologies are human constructions. In an adaptation of a classic Marxist position, the computer and other information technologies can be regarded as the congealed product of communal human labor, *"organs of the human brain, created by the human hand*; the power of knowledge, objectified" (Marx 1866: 706). While not acceding to technological determinism, it must be conceded that the social processes that gave rise to, and sustain, those technologies are not necessarily fully open to imposed modification by institutional or personal will. The human capacities for constructing systems of signs and complex technological artifacts has given rise to information technologies that can be regarded as precursors of and, in some respects, enabling preliminaries for the computer. For instance, the introduction of written language to the Greek world witnessed the development of those analytic activities subsequently differentiated as formal logic and grammar, which were to be significant to the development of the theory of computation (Warner 1994: 55-56). Francis Bacon famously observed, "writing [maketh] an exact man" (Bacon 1597: 209), and without the exactness and systematic control of complexity obtainable from writing and other forms of graphic signification the construction of the computer as machine would seem difficult, if not impossible (see chapter 3). Acknowledging antecedents to modern information technologies prompts the seemingly unasked and unanswered question: is there an origin to graphic communication?

The question itself might seem reminiscent of late nineteenth century teleologies, which sought an origin to their present sophistication. For instance, deliberate semiotic marks were studied in an attempt to determine the origin of writing, and the geological record was read to discover originals to contemporary plant and animal forms, although Darwin's *Origins of Species* only briefly alludes to the origin of humanity (Darwin 1859). In relation to the study of writing, an alphabetical teleology persisted: for instance, David Diringer's comprehensive study regards the alphabet as the "last and most important stage of writing" (Diringer 1968: 13), although it also concedes that precursors to graphic forms regarded as writing can always be found (Diringer 1968: 4). Yet the question also contrasts with such teleologies: it does not seek an origin to graphic communication, but questions whether there is an origin. However, even if an absolute origin is questioned, instances of graphic communication in primarily oral societies without written language are of particular interest. Let us, in this circumscribed space, consider one example, from a text that deals with personages whose "fame is greater than the authenticity of their history" (Voltaire 1764: 16).

Genesis

And God said, Let there be lights in the firmament of the heaven to divide the day from the night; and let them be for signs, and for seasons, and years.

The quotation represents the first explicit allusion to a sign in Genesis. The signs are not iconic, in the sense of there being a resemblance between the sign and what it signifies. Nor are they verbal, either written or spoken. They are natural objects taken as signs: human labor is involved in their recognition and interpretation, not their production. The nature of the signs contrasts with assumptions for historically early or primitive forms of signification, which are sometimes taken to be pictorial, particularly iconic, or verbal and oral. The signs are related to time- rather than space-based functions and could be regarded as analogous in function to the humanly constructed calendars found in primitive cultures (Marschak 1972).

In Genesis, these signs precede the establishment of human society. This sequence could be read to imply a denial of an origin to signification: communication may be a condition of being social or fully human. Although the signs are not verbal, they also carry implications for contrasts commonly made between speech and writing. They suggest a reversal of the commonly assumed or stated historical priority of speech to writing: the signs are analogous in function to notational systems sometimes regarded as forms of writing, or, at least, as precursors of the alphabet. In this context, they precede human, although not divine, speech. Discussions of distinctions between written and spoken language sometimes implicitly appeal to a period of technological innocence, where, for instance speech is naturally impermanent and cannot be preserved by recording. Yet these signs precede the establishment of human society and raise the issue of whether it is legitimate to appeal to a period innocent of external devices for signification. Speech is, then, not naturally impermanent, but impermanent only under specific social and historical conditions. It is also sometimes asserted that the transition from orality to literacy was accompanied by an increase in visual signs, corresponding to the contrast between the graphic nature of writing and the auditory nature of speech. The contrast itself has to be qualified: writing may be relatively consistently graphic (although some forms of writing, such as the matrix of marks on a musical roll or particular transformations of computer programs, may be more readily auditorily than visually intelligible), but speech is only purely auditory if the sounds of utterance are isolated or abstracted from an oral verbal performance. There is some evidence to suggest that such abstraction may be a post-literate move prompted by the development of the idea of language existing apart from a specific verbal performance (see chapter 1). In this context, it should be noted that the first sign in Genesis is visual, not audible.

Conclusion

Why should searching for an origin to graphic communication recall Coleridge's comments on critical attempts to explain Iago's evil, "motive hunting for a motiveless malignity?" Communication is a condition of being social and man is only fully human by being social. Even utilitarian artifacts can assume primarily semiotic functions: Odysseus's final journey was to be concluded when an oar was recognized as a winnowing fan (Warner 1994: 50); in *Strangers on a Train*, a tennis racket signifies a character's profession. Biological individuals, historically, although without empirical validation in Vico's account of human history (Vico 1744) and empirically in confused accounts of savage infants, may be a- or pre-social and, possibly although not necessarily, without signs, but man is always social and necessarily communicating. It may be worth recalling that there is a theological tradition in the human account of Hell, the devils preserve truth among themselves in order better to tempt mankind (Browne 1646: 76).

From these indications of a historical perspective on the development of information technologies, the computer emerges not as a radical novelty but as the product of developments gathering force from the 1870s and 1880s. The associated idea of an abrupt disjunction in the transition to an information society can also be questioned. It may be that current preoccupations with information technologies, and the emerging influence of the recognition of the computer as a universal information machine, have made it possible to regard developments previously considered separately as products of a single human faculty for invention. The idea of an information society, while being questioned insofar as it is taken to imply a radical disjunction, can still be retained as a valuable, and potentially illuminating, investigatory problematic.

Chapter 7

Reviews

Samuel Johnson. *A Dictionary of the English Language on CD-ROM.* **1st (1755) and 4th (1773) editions. Edited by Anne McDermott. Cambridge: Cambridge University Press, 1996.**

This work is the first electronic publication of Johnson's *A Dictionary of the English Language*. It includes both the first (1755) and the fourth (1773) edition (the last to be revised by Johnson), in facsimile and in transcribed form, although Johnson's preface is omitted. The publication embodies a transition that might have interested Johnson as an author concerned with transitions and contrasts between forms of communication, particularly in the preface with differences between written and oral language (Johnson 1755a).

The editorial introduction is unilluminating and possibly derivative (for instance, James Murray's *The Evolution of English Lexicography* (Murray 1900: 35-39) might be a final, if indirect, source for the account of the development of English lexicography (pp. 6-7). The account of the use of the dictionary, not written by the editor, is clear, but the examples of words searched for, such as "knabble" and "funk," are unfortunate—although recognizing this might render oneself liable to Johnson's response to ladies who praised the absence of naughty words: "What! my dears! then you have been looking for them?" (Beste 1829). The omission of the preface limits the possibility of immediate comparison between Johnson's use and definition of words.

The retrieval software allows for standard search facilities, Boolean combinations of terms, and proximity searching, with limitation to particular fields possible. It is based on SGML encoding of the transcribed text. Positively, the standardization offered by SGML allows for future development of the publication. Less satisfactorily, the impression is of retrieval facilities and coding not fully adapted to the underlying structure of the text: for instance, the dictionary entry is not available as a menu driven search category, although it can be distinguished for advanced searching. The example given of an advanced search (pp. 50-52) does not work in practice and inadvertently reveals the penalty of null recall associated with excessive complexity and precision in information retrieval queries. It also draws attention to the inconsistent transcription of Bacon's name as a quoted author: searching for the truncated form "Bacon?" retrieves 9,837 occurrences, "Bacon's" 257, "Bacon" 5,564, and the wildcard form "Bacon?s" 4,273. The apostrophe has been inconsistently transcribed, with an American influenced variant used extensively in the "I" section: only the inconsistent transcription seems to be recalled by the usual form "Bacon's"; the wildcard form "Bacon?s" seems to recall all the consistently transcribed form of "Bacon's" but not the inconsistent transcription; and the truncated form "Bacon?" to recall "Bacon" and the consistently transcribed form of "Bacon's" but, again, not the inconsistent transcription. There would seem to be a combination of inconsistencies in transcription and incomplete matching of query and document characters. Further investigation suggests that the problem occurs with other authors and that care would need to be taken in making estimates of the number of times an author is quoted. Such inconsistencies (and there are other discrepancies) may be a product of haste or inevitable in such an extensive work. For some purposes, such as the close reading of non-Roman alphabets, the resolution offered by the facsimile may not be adequate.

A crucial issue that is not addressed by the editorial introduction is the extent to which the transition to electronic form enables or makes easier new forms of research. One such possibility is the comparison of the definitions given to words as headwords with the use of the defined words in other definitions and in quotations. Their mutual consistency could then be assessed or, perhaps more profitably, the richness of their inevitable inconsistency could be studied, recalling Johnson's own reservations:

> The rigour of interpretative lexicography requires that *the explanation, and the word explained, should be always reciprocal*; this I have always endeavoured but could not always attain.

(Johnson 1755a: 15)

Quoted authors could also be traced and enumerated and their relative use assessed, although both Johnson's use of variant forms (Bac., Bacon, Bacon's and Sh., Sha., Shak., Shakes., Shakesp., Shakespear, Shakspear's, Shakespeare, Shakespeare's) and the vagaries of the transcription and recall procedures would need to be considered, if accuracy and comprehensiveness of recall were desired. The verbal resemblances between the definitions of Johnson's *Dictionary* and those of the *Oxford English Dictionary*, alarmingly frequent and not fully recognized, could also be traced, although this was previously possible by collation between printed editions. The cumulative effect of such possibilities, not exhaustively indicated here, is to add to the potential and richness of the resource.

Understanding the work itself is altered and arguably enhanced by the transition to electronic form. Johnson's own method in constructing entries was to work by analogy and then further to formalize structures and procedures, whereas SGML encoding requires more immediately rigorous systematic analysis. Here, the increased exactness associated with computing can be sensed. Enhanced exactness, in the sense of a capacity for collation difficult or tedious to obtain from printed forms, can also reveal inconsistencies and lacuna in the object studied, with the variant forms of quoted authors' names being readily apparent examples. The physical expressiveness of the book as an artifact, which for this work can acquire a patina and resonance over time, is lost. Becky Sharp's action in *Vanity Fair* when she throws her leaving gift of "Johnson's Dixonary" back to the garden of Miss Pinkerton's academy for young ladies, indicative of her energy and defiance of convention and of her strength (even if an abridged edition is at issue) (Thackeray 1847: 11-16), would lose some of its metaphorical resonance. Yet the transition to electronic form, with the loss of the authority of a folio, can also be liberating, identifying the dictionary as one attempt at description, not a prescriptive monument, even reinvigorating Johnson's original intention to register, rather than form, the language (Johnson 1755a). What might be received as an ahistorical gesture, erasing printed antecedents, can instead be employed to rehistoricize the work. The constraints of the linearity of the printed written form, acutely sensed by Johnson—"When the radical idea branches out into parallel ramifications, how can a consecutive series be formed of senses in their nature collateral?" (Johnson 1755a: 15)—are also partly reduced and cross references are as easily traversed as a linear progression. Cross referencing from transcription to facsimile is marked by a stylized drawing of a camera, exemplifying the conjunction of written verbal with iconic signs, which is becoming increasingly familiar.

In conclusion, this publication offers wide dissemination, with differing means of access, of a work itself rightly considered seminal. The labor omitted in its construction has to be compensated for by care and thought in searching. For full study, both the electronic and printed forms are essential.

Clifford A. Lynch. *Accessibility and Integrity of Networked Information Collections* **(Contractor Report prepared for the Office of Technology Assessment Telecommunication and Computing Technologies Program). Washington, D.C.: Office of Technology Assessment, 1993.**

This report is concerned with networked information access and the integrity of the networked resources available. Information access is explicitly distinguished from network access and this could also be taken to imply a contrast with the focus of public rhetoric on information highways. Integrity of resources, including written, other graphic and audiovisual resources, is generally understood as stability over time or, at least, the possibility of fully recovering diachronic variants. Although the report is historically informed, it does not recall a famous, if not notorious, definition of network:

> **Network**. Any thing reticulated or decussated, at equal distances, with interstices between the intersections.

> (Johnson 1755b)

This definition has, understandably, been criticized for referring the simple to the more complex but could also be read as an allusion to the circularity of signification, as a significant anticipation of the central theme of structuralism, that words obtain their meaning through a network of negative differences. Such an interpretation of the definition does intimate the possibility of a structuralist analysis of networked resources, in which the value of each resource, particularly a bibliographic resource, resides not primarily in itself but in its difference from intellectually proximate, even if geographically scattered, resources. One aspect of the historical connections of network as a term, associated with the interweaving of words and themes in written texts (Barthes 1986) and the rhapsodizing or stitching together of oral poetry (Warner 1994: 50), could also diminish the claims made, which are not uncritically reproduced here, for the radical novelty of networked communication. While recognizing only an arbitrary relation between a sign and what it signifies, and not proposing to substitute etymology for current understanding, these historical precedents do imply the possibility of accommodating and assimilating networked information and might mollify the admittedly rather bleak picture present in the report. Empirical developments and, to some extent, practical understanding of appropriate measures have run ahead of the capacity to give theoretical analyses. It is difficult to generalize without careful qualification and, despite the tendency of network access to erode the significance of geographical distance, there are geopolitical and cultural contrasts. Some distinguishable issues can, however, be considered: the strength of economic influences on developments in networked resources; intellectual property, concentrating on copyright rather than patent; geopolitical and cultural differences themselves; integrity of networked resources; and the extent to which developments are amenable to imposed control.

With regard to economic influences, a crucial distinction that emerges from the report is between economic influences on developments and solutions that might appear economically rational from a system perspective. A further, and also significant, distinction could be between economic rationality from a system perspective and from the viewpoint of the various agents participating in that system. It is conceded that economic rationality from a system viewpoint will not, by itself, determine future patterns: for instance, there is a strong economic justification for the organizational, although not necessarily the technical, centralization of information resources in a networked environment, but the predicted centralization is not occurring. Systemic economic rationality and agreed public policy goals, themselves not necessarily concordant, may conflict with economic influences and market forces: the interests of the various sectors involved, such as commercial publishers, scholarly societies, and libraries, are, in many cases, conflicting and a deliberately and carefully crafted balance among them is required to achieve the desired future. The crucial issue might then be the degree of deliberate control obtainable over partly autonomous and geopolitically dispersed developments. It might be worth recalling that some of the immediate precursors to those technologies that facilitate communication over space, the telephone and the telegraph, gathered force in the late nineteenth century and that their adoption can be plausibly connected with the determining power of the economic base, in this instance with North American continental expansionism and increased connections with Europe.

In relation to copyright, the late nineteenth century also marked the beginnings of a convergence between practices in the United States and other, informationally significant, political regions, although individual reciprocal agreements and changes in domestic practices preceded the much later accession by the United States to the Berne Convention. The idea of the individual author as a figure entitled to economic reward for intellectual labor had emerged toward the end of the eighteenth century and would seem to have survived as much as a rhetorical construction, partly masking corporate interests, as a substantive entity. The relevance of copyright law itself to electronic information is noted to have been diminished, particularly by the substitution of license agreements for copyright provisions. Unless there is a major restructuring of copyright law, and practical developments have tended to run ahead of the products of legislative deliberations, a shift from contract to copyright law seems inexorable. Laws that depart from acceptable norms can tend to be overridden, most obviously in connection with Prohibition, in the case of copyright in electronic information by alternatively available law. An emerging distinction between law as statute and precedent and as a social practice, where it is mediated by common understanding, considerations of cost, including the costs of litigation, and social acceptability analogous to the distinction of imposed economic rationality from economic influences, can be detected. One effect of networked information would seem to be to encourage a further convergence of copyright practices between politically separate domains. With regard to the connection between copyright as intellectual property and legal or copyright deposit, traditionally described as separate but closely related in the United States but not operationally connected in the United Kingdom since 1911, it is urged that enforced, and enforceable, deposit of electronic material with the Library of Congress would help to ensure its long-term accessibility.

In geopolitical terms, networked information is simultaneously global and local, with, for instance, resources locally maintained but globally accessible. Extensive transfer of information across political boundaries could be expected to encourage, and has already led to, erosion of differences in informational practices, particularly where there are reciprocal exchanges of information. Yet there are also contrasts, implied in or detectable from the report, between different regions, with those between the United States and the United Kingdom being most locally relevant. Access to information, and government provision of information, would seem to be more highly valued in the United States. Given the difficulties of imposing change in a relatively liberal culture, the networking of federal information is acknowledged to have a very special role, both as a valuable resource and for the exemplary effect of the availability of such a resource. The influence of the program of foreign acquisitions by the Library of Congress, historically more extensive than that by the British Library, can be detected in the concern expressed that relying on network access to information provided by national libraries and other institutions in foreign countries, rather than acquiring ownership, may lead to a reduction in available information if political policies in the regions concerned change. A cultural contrast, specifically between the commitment of the library and information communities to freedom of access to information and the computing communities, without this traditional commitment and liable to be censorious, is also made. Finally, an irony is detected: that although networks promise largely to eliminate accidents of geography as an organizing principle for institutional cooperation, licensing has the effect that each library becomes an insular, isolated organization, debarred from sharing the licensed resource with other networked organizations. The irony could be further read to imply that the technology does not determine its effects and that, although the situation is complex, economic motivations are influences of greater strength than primarily technical possibilities.

Integrity of resources is primarily understood as stability over time, or, at least, the possibility of reconstructing diachronic variants. Electronic resources are amenable to updating by being overwritten and thereby invite, although they do not compel, an ahistorical view of the world. A partial analogy with forms of discourse significant to oral societies can be adduced: oral genealogies and poetry tended to be changed as they were renewed, when assessed by literate standards of verbatim repetition, although their producers might regard them as invariant. The insistence on the exact replication of the verbal content of written charters, such as the U.S. Constitution, would seem only to be matched by the fluidity of their interpretation. Electronic resources are, with the development of the idea of an exact written and then printed text, regarded as changing. With regard to the exactness associated with written language (see chapter 3), computer-held resources would seem to have an ambivalent effect: encouraging fluidity and change rather than precise replication but simultaneously enabling detailed comparison, including collation, of diachronic variants. The possibility of synchronically coexisting, but geographically dispersed, versions of resources is acknowledged: where written, these resources may again be assuming some of the conditions previously associated with oral rather than written discourse, whereas to transmit and reproduce tends to be to alter. The erosion of the stability of written communication is recognized to extend to other graphic forms, such as photographs in digital formats, and the implications of this are explored. Sight has tended to be a relatively privileged sense in terms of its claim to evidential value, and, to some extent, that value has been allowed to inhere in photographic representations as surrogates for eyewitness testimony. Yet the photographic image in digital form is radically unstable, amenable to alteration without traces of the contrivance, and its status as representation of reality can only be assessed when its provenance and history is known. Visual images may then be assuming the uncertain status of rumor, where the source, not the narrative, is crucial to claims to veracity.

A crucial issue that has emerged as common to these various concerns is the extent to which developments are open to imposed control and direction. There are difficulties in imposition, even when the aim is to preserve or advance relatively agreed values, particularly in liberal cultures: historically, restrictions on the distribution of pornography have been recognized as having social costs and this may be relevant to certain forms of networked information; more immediately apparent is the extent to which economic factors can be more powerful than systemic economic rationality in influencing the development of networked information and law as it is mediated through social practice more significant than law as a formalized code. There would also seem to be some reduction in the autonomy of the nation-state, with regard to networking policy. Given these restrictions on deliberately directing developments, measures open to direct government implementation, such as the networking of federal information, have attractions and a possible exemplary value. The United States, as the apparent leader in the development of networked information, may have a privileged position with its scope for autonomy less restricted by prior developments.

In conclusion, the value of this report would seem to be in enlarging our understanding. If:

> Men make their own history, but not of their own free will; not under circumstances they themselves have chosen but under the given and inherited circumstances with which they are directly confronted.

> (Marx 1852: 146)

then the fuller the understanding of the conditions of making, and of the limitations of autonomy of institutional action and policy, the more fully can the future be directed or, at least, accommodated. The report represents the fullest and most rigorous discussion of the implications of networked information yet encountered, with not all the issues it raises noticed here, and it deserves attention outside the political, and dissolving informational, boundaries of the United States. The lengthy transition the report indicates between printed and electronic form, particularly for primary rather than secondary literature, does give the opportunity to recognize and address the issues raised. It is asserted that networked information can change educational institutions, including lifelong learning, political systems, economic frameworks, and the common culture. Its promise and significance is too great to allow its development to devolve to market influences: conscious, deliberate choices are required and, where necessary, investments to support those choices.

Yorick A. Wilks, Brian M. Slator, and Louise M. Guthrie. *Electric Words: Dictionaries, Computers, and Meanings.* Cambridge, Mass.: MIT Press, 1996.

The title alone of this work could be misleading. It is not an exploration of the epistemological issues raised by attempts to capture meaning in dictionaries or by manipulation of word forms for computer applications. Rather, it is a consideration of the relevance of dictionaries as resources for use in natural language processing (NLP). Epistemological issues, which are introduced, arise largely as a result of this practical endeavor.

The premise that informs the book and some of the work reported is that dictionaries, particularly although not exclusively monolingual dictionaries, constitute an extensive and real-world source of data about the relationship between word forms and meanings. An analogy is drawn with courts and legal processes: both the judiciary and lexicographers take real-world decisions about ethics and about meanings while philosophers debate principles, possibly inconclusively. An indirect inheritance, plausible in a United States context, might be detected from the tradition of attaching value to practical reasoning in legal decisions, associated, for instance, with Oliver Wendell Holmes. A warning as to the viability of using dictionaries as sources for relatively stable meanings could be derived from the historically variable interpretations assigned to verbally unaltered significant legal documents, such as the U.S. Constitution.

The NLP tasks to which meanings obtained from dictionaries are to be applied are not fully enumerated, although they clearly include machine translation, and either may be assumed to be known to the intended communities of readers or, less charitably, could be regarded as poorly defined. The guiding presumption is of the desirability of extensive autonomous computer processing of data and not of frequent human interaction with computer-held data. The coverage of relevant empirical literature seems to be relatively full. The currency of the projects and literature reported is more questionable, with citations diminishing from the late 1980s, and reports of later (1992) projects can descend to rather uncritical itemization without supporting analysis. A slightly more recent (1993) project reported, which takes a user-centered empirical approach in support of machine-assisted translation, for which a database of aligned parallel texts is provided, does contrast with earlier projects in its emphasis on interactivity. The contrast between this and the less interactive approach of other NLP projects discussed should have received greater attention and a full discussion of their relative value would have been helpful. There would seem to be an analogy with current debates in information retrieval, as a move is made from evaluative paradigms developed during an era of batch processing to an attempt to grapple with the current reality of operational systems, which allow a high degree of interaction. The strongest contrast may lie in system intention, to support human exploration and judgment, whether with regard to translation or to document and information retrieval, not in procedures and techniques. The complexity and extent of computer transformations between human interaction may also be diminished.

The framework of understanding brought to the account of NLP projects is sophisticated and widely, although not fully, informed by relevant sources. It recognized that dictionaries are compiled with particular intentions and that applying them to other tasks may be problematic. The messy inconsistency of the world and real-world languages, too diverse for any formal system fully to encompass, is acknowledged. The style of writing is literate and intelligently allusive with a number of references to Samuel Johnson's work as a lexicographer—the occasional misquotation could be regarded as a tribute to Johnson's own practice.

How might the work have been more fully informed? An awareness that the word is a problematic concept in linguistics, not necessarily demarcated in unconstrained oral utterance, and that it can be regarded as a historically developed convention of written language, would have been helpful. Similarly, a fuller sense of the limitations of an undifferentiated concept or plane of meaning and of the possibility of distinguishing between meaning and definition, with meaning always liable to outrun and evade definition, could have contributed. Johnson's own remark, that "to circumscribe poetry by a definition will only show the narrowness of the definer" (Johnson 1781: 752), does indicate an acute awareness of the limitations of lexicography and definition. Equally relevant, if likely to be unfamiliar, are Volosinov's reservations on attempts to construct a semantic unity or even strong coherence for a word: "The various contexts of usage for any one particular word are thought of as forming a series of circumscribed, self-contained utterances all pointed in the same direction. In actual fact, this is far from true. . . . Contexts do not stand side by side in a row, as if unaware of one another, but are in a state of constant tension, or incessant interaction and conflict" (Volosinov 1929: 80). Experience with full text retrieval would seem to be lending empirical confirmation to the theme of the variety of unpredictable contexts and usages for words.[1] With regard to the understanding of formal languages, Wittgenstein's account of the conditions for a logically perfect language in the *Tractatus Logico-Philosophicus*, particularly the insistence that primitive units of that language cannot be known (Wittgenstein 1922), could have been more fully informative.

A fundamental weakness seems to lie in the conception of men as organic entities with symbolic activities (pp. 43-44). A contrasting perspective, associated for instance with the Italian philosopher Giambattista Vico, would be that to be fully human is to be engaged in social communication and signification. Symbolic activities can then only be reified and decontextualized, as they are for forms of NLP, at the expense of reducing or distorting their richness and complexity. Yet the labor invested in creating NLP applications can be adapted to purposes more sympathetic to this perspective. Vico, while rejecting Aristotelian categories as paths for discovery, valued them for the analytical comprehensiveness they could be made to yield, particularly at the beginning of an inquiry: "Aristotle's Categories and Topics are completely useless if one wants to find something new in them. One turns out to be a Llull or Kircher and becomes like a man who knows the alphabet, but cannot arrange the letters to read the great book of nature. But if these tools were considered the indices and ABC's of inquiries about our problem [of certain knowledge] so that we might have it fully surveyed, nothing would be more fertile for research" (Vico 1710: 100-101). Analogously, while rejecting a device such as Wordnet as an account of the stable relations between different word-forms and their meanings, it can still be regarded as valuable for the cognitive control it can be made to yield over an otherwise disordered and amorphous set of entities.

In conclusion, some reservations must be placed on the currency of the work and its lack of full awareness of the contrasts it reveals. For those sympathetic to NLP, it has value as a seemingly comprehensive survey. Those less sympathetic might regard it as partially trapped within an ahistorical notion of information processing whose correspondence to everyday interactive practice has been diminished. It may still be possible to retrieve and transform the labor invested in some NLP applications from such a critical perspective.

Mike Sharples and Thea van der Geest, editors. *The New Writing Environment: Writers at Work in a World of Technology*. Berlin, Heidelberg, New York: Springer Verlag, 1996.

This collection of papers is primarily, although not exclusively, concerned with functional forms of writing, such as reports and documentation produced in a work context. Many of the forms of writing discussed are those that, in Foucault's terms, would not have an author or even a signatory (Foucault 1984). The collection is loosely organized into sections dealing with expanding the idea of writing, writers in new working environments, developments in these environments, and with new, technologically enabled, forms of writing.

The focus of the essays is broadly in accord with a cognitive perspective. It deals with the production or process of writing, rather than its social context or semiological properties. There are some exceptions to this: for instance, Jane Dorner gives a selective account of developments in copyright, which, however, does not take sufficient cognizance of other discussions of the author as an economic beneficiary; Peter Medway provides an interesting treatment of architects' distribution of meaning between oral, written, and other graphic signs in their professional practice.

Some criticisms could be made of the level of focus and other aspects of the essays. A cognitive approach that concentrates on the process of writing tends to take the sign as a given, like ingredients waiting to be assembled into recipes, rather than as something constituted in the process of communication. The concentration on functional forms of writing, while valuable for revealing the pervasiveness of written communication, does exclude more prestigious, and possibly more interesting, forms of writing, such as poetry, fictional narrative, or critical discourse. The process of production of functional and other genres of writing may differ radically, even across the activities of a single biological individual. Writing software documentation, although complex and difficult, may not be painful as the process of writing fiction has been for some authors. Nor may it resemble Fanny Hill's experience (as created by John Cleland): "my pen drops from me here in the extasy now present to my faithful memory!" (Cleland 1749: 183). The possibility of computer programming as form of writing essential to the new technologies discussed is not recognized. Some unfortunate conclusions from the collection as a whole would be that concision and structure are not consensual values, at least as they are exemplified in practice, and that neither is good editorial practice with regard to the treatment of acronyms.

In conclusion, the collection might be valuable to those concerned with facilitating the production of functional forms of writing. For those interested in issues such as the pragmatics of e-mail communication, where the facility and rapidity of oral communication exist without its contextual restraints on indiscretion and without its saving impermanence, or in the influence of changing media on the possibilities of thought, it has, with some exceptions, little to offer.

Brian Kahin and Charles Nesson, editors. *Borders in Cyberspace: Information Policy and the Global Information Infrastructure.* Cambridge, MASS.: MIT Press, 1997.

This collection of papers is concerned with some highly current and significant issues. The preface notes that the experience of geographic space has been transformed by the information revolution and implies that a spatially bound concept of jurisdiction has been inherited. Subsequent papers are concerned, in different ways, with the conflict between these two tendencies, with, for instance, difficulties in determining the location of commercial and criminal acts and with the enforcement of sanctions against extraterritorial persons. The collection seems to have originated from a conference, although full information on this is not given, and it appears to have been subject to light editorial control.

The papers cover a variety of topics within the broad area of concern. David Johnson and David Post discuss the nature of cyberspace and argue that it needs laws and legal institutions of its own. They simultaneously recognize that (in a quotation from a 1909 U.S. judgment) that "All law is *prima facie* territorial" (p. 4). They suggest a password boundary as solution to the problem of enforcement where territorial power does not subsist. Ingrid Volkmer addresses the conflict between cultural sovereignty and global information, pointing to television broadcasting as a precursor to the globalism of the Internet, particularly with regard to the innovation of global programming. Some forms of online provision are noted to have a regional focus. Joel Reidenberg notes that technical standards effectively exert substantial control over information flows and suggests that technical standardization should be deliberately used to achieve regulatory objectives. Christopher Kedzie argues, in a rather tautological presentation, that modern communication and information technologies have a democratic tendency. A. Michael Froomkin deals with the Internet as a source of regulatory arbitrage, the practice of evading disliked domestic regulations by communicating and conducting transactions under regulatory regimes with more favorable rules. Henry Perrit is concerned with jurisdiction in cyberspace and notes that state power has been closely related to judicial authority and that this has historically led to a localization of judicial authority. Dan Burk considers the market for digital piracy, contrasting data piracy with earlier forms of smuggling by reference to the lack of physical substance of data. He also indicates that Internet commerce may not follow conventional models of spatial distribution. Victor Schonberger and Teree Foster discuss free speech and the global information infrastructure, noting that there are inconsistent approaches to restricting freedom of expression, even among Western, democratic, and liberal countries. Robert Gellman deals with the possibility of overlapping rules and of conflict in the areas of privacy regulation (the U.S. term) or data protection (the European equivalent). A survey of encryption is provided by Richard Barth and Clint Smith. Peter Weiss and Peter Backlund deal with the conflict between the exploitation for gain of official information and its provision at least cost and note that different nations have sharply contrasting policies. John Goldring, in the most sophisticated and satisfying paper, "Netting the cybershark: Consumer protection, cyberspace, the nation-state and democracy," does concede that it may be impossible to regulate cyberspace, given the potential geographical mobility of information sources. The collection as a whole appears to be exhaustively indexed.

The papers are informed, both explicitly and implicitly, by some common perspectives. The contributors (with the noticeable exception of John Goldring) are predominantly from a U.S. background and contrast United States/other forms a recurrent basis for comparisons. A tendency to regard law as an autonomously significant artifact, ignoring the relations of power and consent that support it, is detectable. There are also traces of technological determinism, most subtly and pervasively in the limited recognition of information technology as a human construction. Noticeably absent from an information science viewpoint is a bibliographic system perspective, which would identify the reduction of economic constraints on making information public as a crucial contrast between Internet and preexisting forms of publication.

Some criticisms could be made of these perspectives, first in terms of their theoretical and historical awareness, and, second, in terms of the realism of the proposals that arise from these perspectives. It would have been helpful to suggest that we might be witnessing a transposal of classic problems about the nature of money to another domain, to cyberspace. On one classic interpretation, money is the universal equivalent between commodities and, like other commodities, only the material shell of the human labor expended on its production, in this case the production of gold (Marx 1873: 180-198; consider also *The Treasure of the Sierra Madre* (Huston 1948)). Although money can, for certain functions, be replaced by a symbol, it is not a mere symbol: "Hard cash lurks within the ideal measure of value" (Marx 1873: 185 and 198). Certain forms of commerce, reaching their apogee in Internet transactions, accentuate the symbolic aspect of money. A semiotic perspective would identify a crucial issue from a regulatory viewpoint as the possibility of replicating the expression (or signifier) of the symbol with little or uncertain traces of the conditions and location of replication: forgery is enabled and the concept and process of forgery partially transformed. The familiar analogy between money and language in which an item loses or changes its value as it crosses a political or linguistic boundary (Saussure 1916: 117) has also been altered and deserves re-exploration.

The papers reveal a limited historical awareness, for instance, in not discussing the origins of the United States as the creation of a separate jurisdiction, partly motivated by the resentment of taxation imposed by a distant power. It could be further suggested that the violence and relation of power involved in the subsequent development of the United States, including the assimilation of conquest to expansion in the myth and process of Western expansion, has been repressed. Most significantly, relations of power and authority are similarly ignored in the proposal for cyberspace as a jurisdiction: the issue of how sanctions against criminal or undesirable actions are to be enforced is not adequately confronted. The only sanction capable of enforcement would seem to be exclusion from cyberspace conversations (and the excluded entity may be able to assumed a different cyberspace identity) comparable to the territorial punishment of exile.

In conclusion, the papers address significant issues and are highly current in their topics, if less fully historically and theoretically informed. The rapidity of change seems to ensure that changes in practice, which can be accompanied by measures that embody a practical understanding of how to deal with undesirable activities (banishment is already used), will proceed in advance of articulated changes in consciousness. Yet deliberate reflection can inform policy, including the recognition that policies may be most effective as influences and not controls (a recognition that occurs in rather isolated remarks in this collection (pp. 112 and 345). The papers represent a valuable beginning to the process of reflection.

Paul Levinson. *The Soft Edge: A Natural History and Future of the Information Revolution.* **London and New York: Routledge, 1997.**

This work is about "the difference that communications media make in our lives" (p. xi). It has a broad historical scope, ranging from the development of the alphabet to the future of artificial intelligence, and it takes a non-technical approach. Its scope and perspective promise great interest.

There are a number of isolated *apercus*. We learn that in ancient Greece democracy was defined by the extent to which an audience could hear a speaker's voice, although the implied congruence between a discourse and speech community is not noticed. Nathaniel Hawthorne's 1851 comment on the telegraph is quoted: "Is it a fact—or have I dreamed it—that, by means of electricity, the world of matter has become a great nerve vibrating thousands of miles in a breathless point of time?" (p. 127). The possibility implied by the date and geopolitical context of the quotation that the mid- to late nineteenth century represents the crucial period for the adoption of technologies subsequently subsumed under the generic term *information technology*, and that they were produced by the demands of United States continental expansion for communication across space, is not explored. The quotation is indicative of the perspective assumed, which is from the United States, with little deep sense of the possibility of other cultural perspectives on information developments.

The historical range of reference of the work is not matched by a deeper historical understanding. For instance, it is asserted that no group without writing has achieved a civilization: Homeric and other sophisticated, primarily oral cultures provide counter examples. The treatment of the development of copyright is particularly unsatisfactory. For Levinson, the "biological antiquity of property . . . is no doubt what led to the development of provisions for intellectual property when the printing press for the first time put such property in the form of books of everyone's shelf" (pp. 202-203). Yet non-U.S. cultures, most notably feudal and Marxist ones, have valued copying and dissemination above personal property rights, if these were even acknowledged—for instance, Chinese printing, whose early development is remarked by Levinson, did not give rise to Western concepts of copyright. The transformation of copyright from a printers' to an author's right in the late eighteenth and early nineteenth centuries is seen as a correction and not as a transformation, which could be connected to the concurrent emergence of the Romantic conception of the author as a creative individual. Significant potentially highly relevant sources are neglected in discussions of other topics: for instance, considerations of orality and of the history of writing show no awareness of the classic work of Diringer or the more recent studies by Ong, Gaur, and Harris.

There are also theoretical limitations. The distinction between natural and humanly made artifacts is obscured in the proposal for the further development of "evolutionary epistemology," which would study the analogies between "the evolution of biological organisms and the evolution of human knowledge" (p. xvi). While there may be analogies in patterns of development, the mechanisms are radically different (except in the curious and significant cases of selective breeding and genetic engineering), one an effect of nature, the other the product of human intellectual labor. There is a correspondingly limited recognition of technology as a human construction. The crucial distinction between invention and innovation (or social diffusion) is hinted at but not consistently developed. A causal role is attributed to information technology developments: the alphabet is regarded as an influence toward monotheism, not simply as a carrier for its dissemination; and capitalism implied to be a product of the printing press. In summary, the approach implied by Walter Benjamin's remark that, "within the phenomenon [of the possibilities of reproduction of art objects] which we are here examining from the perspective of world history, print is merely a special, though particularly important, case" (Benjamin 1936: 219) is partly realized through the scope of historical reference. The associated, and persuasive, position, which gives full primacy to the economic and cultural over the technological, that the adoption of printing and the wider dissemination of texts was a product of the stress on personal conscience in Protestantism, is not explored.

The method of argument tends to be that of assertion—the phrase "no doubt" recurs to link questionable causalities. The style itself has the fluidity characteristic of spoken delivery, as well as some more clearly marked oral linguistic features, and the rapid transition between topics also found in compilations of short pieces. The subtlety of sources can be obscured: in the discussion of Socrates' objections to writing as inert and unresponsive, it is not noted that similar objections are made to oral communication delivered as a speech rather than dialectically engaged; Frankenstein's status as a victim of human conduct in Mary Shelley's narrative, as well as when represented by Boris Karloff, is not noticed; and, most crucially, the reservations on free speech as undivided good made in classical liberal discussions (which, for instance, attend to the time and place of utterances and do not condone incitement to riot) are neglected.

In conclusion, the scope and ease of reading of the work make it valuable, despite its deeper deficiencies. Its broader value could be said to lie in its failure to fulfill its intentions: it simultaneously exposes an interesting area and the need to occupy that area coherently and intelligently.

Notes

Chapter 4. Toward an Integrated Account of Formal Logic and Automata Theory: Iconic and Notational Models

1. The literature of automata studies is profuse. References have been deliberately restricted. For a recent authoritative survey, see Herken 1995.

A similar restraint in giving references has been observed with regard to the literature of formal logic.

2. The discussion here implies that an unlimited symbol space is sufficient for both growing and infinite automata. This is intended as an acceptable simplification of a complex issue that would seem to have a parallel in debates with philosophy and mathematics on whether infinity is substantively different from number. The position implicitly endorsed here is that indicated by Vico, namely, that human constructions can be only nominally infinite:

> The truth is that those genera are only nominally infinite, since man is neither nothing nor everything. Consequently, he cannot think about nothing, except by the negation of something; nor can he think about the infinite except by the negation of the finite.
>
> These sciences create the truths they teach. Man contains within himself a fictitious world of lines and numbers, and he operates in it with his abstractions just as God operates with reality.

(Vico 1744: 63 and 123)

3. For examples of the computational process that inform the discussion of its semiotic aspects and the methodology of construction of the Turing machine, see Warner 1994; Penrose 1989; Davis, 1982; Boolos and Jeffrey 1989; Sommerhalder and Westrhenen 1988.

Chapter 5. Writing and Literary Work in Copyright: A Binational and Historical Analysis

1. The rhyme would appear to be a mnemonic for two forms, or precisely, moods, of the Aristotelian syllogism (Bochenski 1961: 40-99).

Chapter 7. Reviews

1. I cite, but do not reproduce, the recall of an article discussing a new translation of the *Kama Sutra* from the full text file of *The Guardian* (London) (1992) by the logical combination "university" AND "library" AND "finance."

Bibliography

Abrams, H. B. (1991). *The law of copyright*. New York: Clark Boardman Company.

Ager v. Peninsula. (1884). Ager v. Peninsula and Oriental Steam Company. *The Law reports: Chancery division*, xxvi, 637-643.

Ager v. Collingridge. (1886). Ager v. Collingridge. *Times*. February 4, 1886, 3.

Anderson v. Lieber. (1917). D. P. Anderson and Co. Limited v. Lieber Code Company. *The Times law reports*, xxxiii, 1916-1917, 420-421.

Apple v. Franklin. (1982). Apple Computer Inc. v. Franklin Computer Corp. United States Court of Appeals, Third Circuit, 1983. 714 F. 2d. 1240. In M. B. Nimmer. *Cases and materials on copyright and other aspects of entertainment litigation including unfair competition, defamation, privacy* (pp. 124-133). 4th edition, 1991. St. Paul, Minn.: West Publishing.

Aristotle (323 BCa). *The ethics of Aristotle: The Nicomachean ethics*. Translated by J. A. K. Thomson. Revised with notes and appendices by Hugh Tredennick. Introduction and bibliography by Jonathan Barnes, 1976. London: Penguin Group.

Aristotle. (323 BC). *Categories and De interpretatione*. Translated with notes by J. L. Ackrill, 1989. Oxford: Clarendon Press.

Bacon, F. (1597). Of studies. In F. Bacon. *The essays* (pp.209-210). Edited with an introduction by John Pitcher, 1985. New York: Penguin Books.

Bar-Hillel, Y. (1955). An examination of information theory. In Y. Bar-Hillel. *Language and information: Selected essays on their theory and application*. 1964. Reading, Mass.: Addison-Wesley, and Jerusalem: Jerusalem Academic Press.

Barthes, R. (1986). From work to text. In R. Barthes. *The rustle of language* (pp. 56-64). Oxford: Basil Blackwell.

Bavel, Z. (1991). *Introduction to the theory of automata.* 2nd edition. Reston, Va.: Reston Publishing Company.

Beeson, M. J. (1995). Computerizing mathematics: Logic and computation. In R. Herken (Ed.), *The universal Turing machine: A half-century survey* (pp. 173-205). 2nd edition. New York: Springer-Verlag.

Bell, D. (1980). The social framework of the information society. In T. Forester (Ed.). *The microelectronics revolution: The complete guide to the new technology and its impact on society* (pp. 500-549). Oxford: Basil Blackwell.

Benjamin, W. (1936). The work of art in the age of mechanical reproduction. In W. Benjamin. *Illuminations* (pp. 217-251). Edited by H. Arendt and translated by H. Zohn, 1969. New York: Schocken Books.

Berger, P. L. and Luckmann, T. (1985*). The social construction of reality.* Harmondsworth: Penguin Books.

Berlin Convention. (1908). *Convention of Berlin.* In F. E. Skone James. *Copinger and Skone James on the law of copyright including international and colonial copyright, with the statutes relating thereto and forms and precedents* (pp. 437-458). 1948. London: Sweet and Maxwell.

Berne Convention. (1886). *Berne Convention of September 9th, 1886.* In F. E. Skone James. *Copinger on the law of copyright* (pp. 397-422). 6th edition, 1927. London: Sweet and Maxwell.

Beste, H. D. (1829). *Personal and literary memorials.* In J. L. Sutherland (Ed.). *The Oxford book of literary anecdotes* (p. 86.). 1976. London: Oxford University Press.

Biber, D. (1988). *Variation across speech and writing.* Cambridge: Cambridge University Press.

Boas, F. (1911). Introduction to *Handbook of American Indian languages.* In F. Boas. *Introduction to Handbook of American Indian languages* [and] J. W. Powell. *Indian linguistic families of America north of Mexico* (pp. 1-79). Edited by P. Holder, 1991. Lincoln: University of Nebraska Press.

Bochenski, I. M. (1961). *History of formal logic.* Translated and edited by Ivo Thomas. South Bend, Ind.: Notre Dame University Press.

Boole, G. (1854). *An investigation of the laws of thought, on which are founded the mathematical theories of logic and probabilities.* London: Walton and Maberly. Cambridge: Macmillan.

Boolos, G. S. and Jeffrey, R. C. (1989). *Computability and logic.* 3rd edition. Cambridge: Cambridge University Press.

Boosey v. Whight. (1899). Boosey v. Whight. Appeal from the Chancery division. Dec. 4, 5, and 13, 1899 (before Lindley, M.R., Sir Francis Jeune, and Romer, L.J.). *The Law Times Reports,* LXXXI, 571-575.

Brett, H. and Perry, L. (1981). Introduction: Technical background–legal background. In L. Perry and H. Brett (Eds.). *The legal protection of computer software* (pp. 1-29). Oxford: ESC Publishing.

Brown, A. D. (1987). *Towards a theoretical information science: Information science and the concept of a paradigm.* Sheffield: University of Sheffield, Department of Information Studies

Browne, T. (1646). *Pseudoxia epidemica.* In G. Keynes (Ed.). *The works of Sir Thomas Browne* (Volume II). 1964, London: Faber and Faber.

Brussels Convention. (1948). *Brussels copyright convention 1948.* In F. E. Skone James and E. P. Skone James. *Copinger and Skone James on the law of copyright including international and colonial copyright, with the statutes relating thereto and forms and precedents* (paragraphs 675-703). 1965. London: Sweet and Maxwell.

Buckland, M. K. (1997). What is a "document"? *Journal of the American Society for Information Science* 48, 804-809.

Burn, A. R. (1972). Introduction. In Herodotus. *The histories* (pp. ix-xxviii). Translated by A. de Selincourt and revised by A. R. Burn. London: Penguin Books.

Cherry, C. (1957). *On human communication: A review, a survey, and a criticism.* 3rd edition. 1978. Cambridge, Mass.: MIT Press.

Church, A. (1936). An unsolvable problem of elementary number theory. In M. Davis (Ed.). *The undecidable: Basic papers on undecidable propositions, unsolvable problems and computable functions* (pp. 89-107). 1965. Hewlett, N.Y.: Raven Press. First published in *The American Journal of Mathematics.* 58, 345-363.

Cleland, J. (1749). *Memoirs of a woman of pleasure*. Edited with an introduction and notes by Peter Sabor, 1985. Oxford: Oxford University Press.

CONTU. (1978). *Final report of the National Commission on New Technological Uses of Copyrighted Works*. Washington, D.C.: The Commission.

Copyright Act. (1710). *An act for the encouragement of learning, by vesting the copies of printed books in the authors or purchasers of such copies, during the times therein mentioned*. 1709, 8 Anne Ch. xix.

Copyright Act. (1790). *An act for the encouragement of learning by securing the copies of maps, charts, and books, to the authors and proprietors of such copies, during the time therein mentioned*. May 31, 1790. First Congress. Sess. II. Ch. 15.

Copyright Act. (1842). *An act to amend the law of copyright 1842*. 5 and 6 Victoria Ch. xlv.3.

Copyright Act. (1865). *An act supplemental to an act entitled "An act to amend the several acts respecting copyright," approved February third, eighteen hundred and thirty-one, and to the acts in addition thereto and amendment thereof*. March 3, 1965. Thirty-eighth Congress. Sess. II. Ch. 126.

Copyright Act. (1867). *An act amendatory of the several acts respecting copyrights*. February 13, 1867. Thirty-ninth Congress. Sess. II. Ch. 43.

Copyright Act. (1870). *An act to revise, consolidate, and amend the statutes relating to patents and copyrights*. July 8, 1870. Forty-first Congress. Sess. II. Ch. 230.

Copyright Act. (1882). *An act to amend the statutes in relation to copyright*. August 1, 1882. Forty-seventh Congress. Session I. Ch. 366.

Copyright Act. (1891). *An act to amend title sixty, chapter three, of the revised statutes of the United States, relating to copyrights*. March 3, 1891. Fifty-first Congress. Sess. II. Ch. 565.

Copyright Act. (1909). *An act to amend and consolidate the acts respecting copyright*. March 4, 1909. Sixtieth Congress. Sess. II. Ch. 320.

Copyright Act. (1911). *Copyright Act 1911*. 1 and 2 George V. Ch. 46.

Copyright Act. (1956). *Copyright Act 1956*. 4 and 5 Eliz. 2. Ch. 74.

Copyright Act. (1976). *General revision of the copyright law*. October 19, 1976. Public Law 94-553. U.S.C. § 101. Title 17.

Copyright Act. (1980). *An act to amend the patent and trademark laws*. December 12, 1980. Public Law 96-517. 94 STAT. 3028.

Copyright Act. (1985). *Copyright (Computer software) Amendment Act 1985*. Elizabeth II c. 41.

Copyright Act. (1988). *Copyright, designs and patents Act 1988*. Elizabeth II c. 48.

Copyright and designs. (1977). *Copyright and designs law: Report of the committee to consider the laws on copyright and designs, chairman the honourable Mr Justice Whitford* (Cmnd 6732). London: Her Majesty's Stationery Office.

Current law. (1989). *Current law statutes annotated: 1988*. Vol. 4. London: Sweet and Maxwell and Stevens and Sons; Edinburgh: W. Green and Son.

Darwin, C. (1859). *The origin of species by means of natural selection or The preservation of favoured races in the struggle for life*. Edited by J. W. Burrow, 1968. London: Penguin Group.

Davis, M. (1965). *The undecidable: Basic papers on undecidable propositions, unsolvable problems and computable functions*. Hewlett, N.Y.: Raven Press.

———. (1982). *Computability and unsolvability*. New York: Dover Publications.

———. (1988). Mathematical logic and the origin of modern computing. In R. Herken (Ed). *The universal Turing machine: A half-century survey* (pp. 135-158). 2nd edition 1995. New York: Springer-Verlag.

Derrida, J. (1976). *Of grammatology*. Translated by G. C. Spivak. Baltimore: John Hopkins University Press.

Dickens, C. (1861). *Great expectations*. 1991. London: Mandarin.

Dijkstra, E. W. (1989). On the cruelty of really teaching computer science (The SIGCSE Award Lecture 1989). *SIGCSE Bulletin: A Quarterly Publication of the Special Interest Group on Computer Science Education* 21, xxiv-xxxix.

Diringer, D. (1968). *The alphabet: A key to the history of mankind*. 2 volumes. 3rd edition revised with the collaboration of R. Regensburger. London: Hutchison.

Dworkin, G. (1984). The nature of computer programs. In J. Lahore, G. Dworkin, and Y. M. Smyth (Eds.). *Information technology: The challenge to copyright* (pp. 89-114). London: Sweet and Maxwell.

Eco, U. (1976). *A theory of semiotics*. Bloomington: Indiana University Press.

Encyclopaedia Britannica. (1910). Dualla. In *Encyclopaedia Britannica,* volume 8, p. 614. 11th edition. Cambridge: Cambridge University Press.

Finnegan, R. (1970). *Oral literature in Africa.* Oxford: Clarendon Press.

_____. (1989). Communication and technology. *Language and Communication* 9, 107-127.

Fleck, L. (1979). *Genesis and development of a scientific fact.* Edited by T. J. Trenn and R. K. Merton, translated by F. Bradley and T. J. Treen. Chicago: University of Chicago Press.

Flint, M. F. (1985). *A user's guide to copyright.* 2nd edition. London: Butterworths.

Foucault, M. (1984). What is an author? In P. Rabinow (Ed.). *The Foucault reader* (pp. 101-120). Harmondsworth: Penguin Books.

Gandy, R. (1995). The confluence of ideas in 1936. In R. Herken (Ed.). *The universal Turing machine: A half-century survey* (pp. 51-102), 2nd edition. New York: Springer-Verlag.

Gaur, A. (1992). *A history of writing.* Revised edition. New York.: Cross River Press.

Gödel, K. (1946). Remarks before the Princeton bicentennial conference on problems in mathematics. In M. Davis (Ed.). *The undecidable: Basic papers on undecidable propositions, unsolvable problems and computable functions* (pp. 84-88). 1965. Hewlett, N.Y.: Raven Press.

*Goldstein v. Californ*ia. (1973). Donald Goldstein et. al., Petitioners *v.* State of California (United States Supreme Court–Argued Dec. 13, 1972–Decided June 18, 1972). 93. S. Ct. 2303; 412 U.S. 546; 37 L. Ed. 2d 163; 178 USPQ 129. In *Decisions of the United States courts involving copyright* (Copyright Office Bulletin No. 39) (pp. 246-268). 1976. Washington, D.C.: Copyright Office, Library of Congress.

Goody, J. (1977). *The domestication of the savage mind.* Cambridge: Cambridge University Press.

Goody, J. and Watt, I. (1963). The consequences of literacy. In J.

Goody (Ed.). *Literacy in traditional societies*. 1968. Cambridge: Cambridge University Press.

Graves, R. (1960). *The Greek myths*. London: Penguin Books.

Griffith, F. L. (1911). Thoth. In *Encyclopaedia Britannica*. volume 26, pp. 881-882. 11th edition. Cambridge: Cambridge University Press.

Harris, R. (1986). *The origin of writing*. London: Duckworth.

_____. (1989). How does writing restructure thought? *Language and Communication* 9, 99-106.

_____.(1995). *Signs of writing*. New York: Routledge.

Hasan, R. (1987). Directions from structuralism. In N. Fabb, D. Attridge, A. Durant, and C. MacCabe (Ed.). *The linguistics of writing: Arguments between language and literature* (pp. 103-122). Manchester: Manchester University Press.

Havelock, E. A. (1982). *The literate revolution in Greece and its cultural consequences*. Princeton, N.J.: Princeton University Press.

Henderson, M. H. (1983). Protecting computer programs. *American Society for Information Science Bulletin* 9, 5.

Herken, R. (1995). *The universal Turing machine: A half-century survey*. 2nd edition. New York: Springer-Verlag.

Herodotus. (430 BC). *The histories*. Translated by A. de Selincourt and revised by A. R. Burn. London: Penguin Books, 1972.

Holland, M. J. (1978). A brief history of American copyright law. In Herbert S. White (Ed.). *The copyright dilemma* (Proceedings of a conference held at Indiana University, April 14-15, 1977) (pp. 3-26). Chicago: American Library Association.

Huston, J. (1948). *The treasure of the Sierra Madre* [Film]. Los Angeles, Calif.: Warner Bros.

Jenkins v. News Syndicate. (1926). Jenkins v. News Syndicate Co. Inc. (Supreme Court, New York County. Nov. 5, 1926). 219 N.Y. Supp. 196; 128 Misc. Rep. 284. In Library of Congress. Copyright Office. *Decisions of the United States courts involving copyright 1924-1935* (Copyright Office Bulletin No. 20) (pp. 341-344). Washington, D.C.: Government Printing Office, 1936.

Johnson, S. (1755a). Preface to the Dictionary. In E. L. McAdam and G. Milne (Eds.). *Johnson's dictionary: A modern selection* (pp. 3-29). London: Macmillan, 1982.

——— (1775b). A dictionary of the English language. 1818. London: Lonagman.

———— (1781). Life of Pope. In D. Greene (Ed.). *Samuel Johnson* (The Oxford Authors). 1984. (pp. 725-752). Oxford: Oxford University Press.

Johnson-Laird, P. N. (1993). *The computer and the mind: An introduction to cognitive science.* 2nd edition. London: Fontana.

Kirk, G. S. (1985). *The Iliad: A commentary.* Volume I: books 1-4. Cambridge: Cambridge University Press.

Kleene, S. C. (1935). General recursive functions of natural numbers (Presented to the American Mathematical Society, September 1935). In M. Davis (Ed.). *The undecidable: Basic papers on undecidable propositions, unsolvable problems and computable functions.* 1965. Hewlett, N.Y.: Raven Press.

Kneale, W. K. and Kneale, M. (1962). *The development of logic.* Oxford: Clarendon Press.

Kuhn, T. S. (1970). *The structure of scientific revolutions.* 2nd edition. Chicago: University of Chicago Press.

Leith, P. (1990). *Formalism in AI and computer science.* New York: Ellis Horwood.

Lord, A. B. (1960). *The singer of tales.* Cambridge Mass.: Harvard University Press; London: Oxford University Press.

Lynch, M. F. (1977). Variety generation: A reinterpretation of Shannon's Mathematical Theory of Communication, and its implications for information science. *Journal of the American Society for Information Science* 28, 19-25.

Lyotard, J.-F. (1984). *The postmodern condition: a report on knowledge.* Translated by G. Bennington and B. Masumi. Manchester: Manchester University Press.

Mackenzie, D. (1996). *Knowing machines: Essays on technical change.* Cambridge, Mass.: MIT Press.

Mai, J. E. (1997). The concept of subject in a semiotic light. In C. Schwarz and M. Rorvig (Eds). *Proceedings of the 60th ASIS annual meeting* (pp. 54-64). Medford, N.J.: Information Today.

Marschak, A. (1972). *The roots of civilization: The cognitive beginnings of man's first art, symbol and notation.* London: Weidenfeld and Nicholson.

Marx, K. (1852). The eighteenth Brumaire of Louis Bonaparte. In K. Mark. *Surveys from exile: Political writings* (Volume 2, pp. 143-249). Edited by David Fernbach, 1973. Harmondsworth: Penguin Books in association with New Left Review.

_____. (1866). *Grundrisse: Foundations of the critique of political economy* (Rough draft). Translated with a Foreword by Martin Nicolaus, 1993. London: Penguin Books in association with New Left Review.

_____. (1873). *Capital: A critique of political economy.* Volume One. Introduced by Ernest Mandel and translated by Ben Fowkes, 1976. Harmondsworth: Penguin Books in association with New Left Review.

McKenzie, D. F. (1986). *Bibliography and the sociology of texts* (Panizzi Lectures 1985). London: British Library.

_____.(1990). Speech-manuscript-print. *The library chronicle of the University of Texas* 20, 87-109.

Miller, J. K. (1981). *U.S. copyright documents: An annotated collection for use by educators and librarians.* Littleton, Colo.: Libraries Unlimited.

Minsky, M. L. (1967). *Computation: Finite and infinite machines.* Englewood Cliffs, N.J.: Prentice-Hall.

Murray, J. A. H. (1900). *The evolution of English lexicography.* 1970. College Park, Md.: McGrath Publishing Company.

Niblett, B. (1980). *Legal protection of computer programs.* London: Oyez Publishing.

Nimmer, D. (1990). *Nimmer on copyright: Computer law, software protection, intellectual property counseling & litigation, and entertainment industry contracts; the Berne Convention Implementation Act of 1988.* New York: M. Bender.

OED (1989). *The Oxford English dictionary.* 2nd edition. Prepared by J. A. Simpson and E. S. C. Weiner. Oxford: Clarendon Press.

Ong, W. J. (1982). *Orality and literacy: The technologizing of the word.* London: Methuen.

_____. (1986). Writing is a technology that restructures thought. In G. Baumann (Ed.). *The written word: Literacy in transition* (Wolfson College Lectures 1985) (pp. 23-50). Oxford: Clarendon Press.

Penrose, R. (1989). *The emperor's new mind: Concerning computers, minds, and the laws of physics.* Oxford: Oxford University Press.

Phillips, J. (1986). *Introduction to intellectual property law.* London: Butterworths.

Pitman v. Hines. (1884). Pitman v. Hines. *Times.* November 6, 1884, p. 3.

Plato. (385 BC). *Meno*. In Plato. *Protagoras and Meno*. Translated by W. K. C. Guthrie. London: Penguin Books.

———.(400 BC). *Phaedrus*. In Plato. *Phaedrus and the seventh and eighth letters*. Translated and introduced by W. Hamilton, 1973. Harmondsworth: Penguin Books.

Plutarch (100). Life of Theseus. In Plutarch. *The rise and fall of Athens: Nine Greek lives by Plutarch* (pp. 13-41). 1960. Translated and introduced by I. Scott-Kilvert. Harmondsworth: Penguin Books.

Post, E. L. (1936). Finite combinatory processes. Formulation 1. In M. Davis (Ed.). *The undecidable: Basic papers on undecidable propositions, unsolvable problems and computable functions* (pp. 289-291). 1965. Hewlett, N.Y.: Raven Press.

Quine, W. V. O. (1953). New foundations for mathematical logic. In W. V. O. Quine. *From a logical point of view: Logico-philosophical essays* (pp. 80-101). Cambridge, Mass.: Harvard University Press.

Ramsey, F. P. (1926a). The foundations of mathematics. In F. P. Ramsey. *Foundations: Essays in philosophy, logic, mathematics and economics* (pp. 152-212). Edited by D. H. Mellor, 1978. London: Routledge and Kegan Paul.

———.(1926b). Truth and probability. In F. P. Ramsey. *Philosophical papers* (pp. 54-94). Edited by. D. H. Mellor, 1990. London and Henley: Routledge and Kegan Paul.

Rayward-Smith, V. J. (1986). *A first course in computability*. Oxford: Blackwell Scientific.

Reiss v. National Quotation Bureau. (1921). Reiss v. National Quotation Bureau (Inc.) (District Court, S.D. New York, November 15, 1921). 276 Fed. Rep. 717. In Library of Congress Copyright Office. *Decisions of the United States courts involving copyright: 1918-1924* (Copyright Office Bulletin No.19) (pp. 345-348). 1926. Washington, D.C.: G.P.O..

Ringer, B. (1974). The demonology of copyright. In B. H. Weil and B. F. Polansky (Eds.). *Modern copyright fundamentals: Key writings on technological and other issues* (pp. 24-28). New York: Van Nostrand Reinhold, 1985. First published *Publishers' Weekly* 206 (21), 1974, 26-30.

Rose, A. C. (1982). Protection of intellectual property rights in computers and computer programs: Recent developments. In Ben H. Weil and Barbara Friedman Polansky (Eds). *Modern copyright fundamentals: Key writings on technological and other issues* (pp.

266-276). New York: Van Nostrand Reinhold, 1985. First published *Pepperdine Law Review* 9 (3), 1982, 546-569.

Rousseau, J.-J. (1755). Essay on the origin of languages. In Jean-Jacques Rousseau. *Essay on the origin of languages* [and] Johan Gottfried Herder. *Essay on the origin of language*. Translated by A. Gode and J. Moran, 1966. Chicago: University of Chicago Press.

Russell, B. (1922). Introduction. In L. Wittgenstein. *Tractatus logico-philosophicus*. 1988. London: Routledge and Kegan Paul.

Ryle, G. (1949). *The concept of mind*. 1988. Harmondsworth: Penguin Books.

Saussure, F. de (1916). *Course in general linguistics*. Edited by C. Bally and A. Sechehaye with the collaboration of A. Riedlinger, translated and annotated by R. Harris, 1983. London: Duckworth.

Schmandt-Besserat, D. (1978). The earliest precursor of writing. *Scientific American 238*, 6: 38-47.

Shannon, C. E. and Weaver, W. (1949). *The mathematical theory of communication*. Urbana: University of Illinois Press.

Shannon, C. E. and McCarthy, J. (1956). *Automata studies*. Princeton, N.J.: Princeton University Press.

Shera, J. H. (1952). Foundations of a theory of bibliography. In J. H. Shera. *Libraries and the organization of knowledge* (pp. 18-33). Edited by D.J. Foskett, 1965. Hamden, Conneticut: Archon Books. First published *Library Quarterly*. 22, 125-137.

Shera, J. H. (1961). Social epistemology, general semantics, and librarianship. In J.H. Shera. *Libraries and the organization of knowledge* (pp. 12-17). Edited by D. J. Foskett, 1965. Hamden, Conn.: Archon Books. First published *Wilson Library Bulletin* 35. 767-770.

Shields, M. W. (1987). *An introduction to automata theory*. Oxford: Blackwell Scientific.

Skone James, F. E. (1948). *Copinger and Skone James on the law of copyright including international and colonial copyright, with the statutes relating thereto and forms and precedents*. London: Sweet and Maxwell.

Skone James, F. E. and Skone James, E. P. (1965). *Copinger and Skone James on copyright including international copyright, with the statutes and orders relating thereto and forms and precedents and related forms of protection*. London: Sweet and Maxwell.

Skone James E. P., Mummery, J. F., Rayner James, J. E., Latman, A., and Silman, S. (1980). *Copinger and Skone James on copyright including international copyright, with the statutes and orders relating thereto and forms and precedents and related forms of protection.* London: Sweet and Maxwell.

Sommerhalder, R. and Van Westrhenen, S. C. (1988). *The theory of computability: programs, machines, effectiveness and feasibility.* Wokingham, England: Addison-Wesley.

Sperber, D. and Wilson, D. (1986). *Relevance: Communication and cognition.* Oxford: Basil Blackwell.

Thackeray, W. P. (1848). *Vanity fair: A novel without a hero.* Edited by G. Tillotson and K. Tillotson, 1963. London: Methuen.

Turing, A. M. (1937). On computable numbers, with an application to the *Entscheidungsproblem* (Paper read November 12, 1936*). Proceedings of the London Mathematical Society* 42, 230-265.

————.(1950). Computing machinery and intelligence. In A. R. Anderson (Ed.). *Minds and machines* (pp. 4-30). 1964. Englewood Cliffs, N.J.: Prentice-Hall. First published, *Mind.* 59, 433-460.

Twain, M. (1875). Some learned fables for good old boys and girls. In C. Neider, (Ed.). *The complete short stories of Mark Twain* (pp. 104-121). New York: Bantam Books.

U.S. Congress. Office of Technology Assessment. (1986). *Intellectual property rights in an age of electronics and information* (OTA-CIT-302). Washington, D.C.: Government Printing Office.

U.S. Constitution. (1789). The Constitutional provision concerning copyright. In M. B. Nimmer. *Nimmer on copyright : A treatise on the law of literary, musical and artistic property, and the protection of ideas* (Appendix 1). 1963-1991. Albany, N.Y.: M. Bender.

U.S. House of Representatives. (1976). *Report No. 94-1976: Copyright law revision.* Washington, D.C.: Government Printing Office.

Universal Copyright Convention. (1952). *Universal Copyright Convention.* In E. P. Skone James. *Copinger and Skone James on copyright including international copyright with the statutes and orders relating thereto and forms and precedents* (paragraphs 1730-1756). 11th edition, 1971. London: Sweet and Maxwell.

Vico, G. (1710). *On the most ancient wisdom of the Italians: Unearthed from the origins of the Latin language: including the disputation with the Giornale de' letterati d'Italia.* Translated and introduced by L. M. Palmer, 1988. Ithaca, N.Y.: Cornell University Press.

_____.(1725) *The autobiography of Giambattista Vico.* Translated by M.H. Fisch and T.G. Bergin, 1944. Ithaca and London: Cornell University Press.

_____.(1744). *The new science of Giambattista Vico.* Unabridged translation of the third edition (1744) with the addition of "Practic of the New Science" by T. G. Bergin and M. H. Fisch, 1976. Ithaca, N.Y.: Cornell University Press.

Volosinov, V. N. (1929). *Marxism and the philosophy of language.* Translated by L. Matejka and I. R. Titunik, 1973. New York: Seminar Press.

Voltaire (1764). Abraham. In Voltaire *Philosophical dictionary.* Edited and translated by T. Besterman, 1972. London: Penguin Books.

Walter v. Lane. (1900). Walter v. Lane. *Times Law Reports. 16,* 551-556.

Wang, H. (1960). Towards mechanical mathematics. *IBM Journal of Research and Development.* 4: 2-22.

Wang, H. (1974). *From mathematics to philosophy.* London: Routledge and Kegan Paul.

Warner, J. (1990). Semiotics, information science, documents and computers. *Journal of Documentation* 46, 16-32

————.(1994). *From writing to computers.* London: Routledge.

————.(1999). An information view of history. *Journal of the American Society for Information Science 12,* 1125-1126.

Whitehead, A. N. and Russell, B. (1913). *Principia mathematica to *56.* 2nd edition, 1962. Cambridge: Cambridge University Press.

White-Smith v. Apollo. (1908). White-Smith Music Pub. Co. v. Apollo Co. United States Supreme Court–Argued January 16, 17, 1908–Decided February 24, 1908). 209 U.S.I. 28 S. Ct. 319 52 L. Ed. 655. In *Decisions of the United States courts involving copyright and literary property* (Copyright Office Bulletin No. 15) (pp. 2978-2986). 1909. Washington, D.C.: Copyright Office, Library of Congress.

Wiener, N. (1954). *The human use of human beings: Cybernetics and society.* Revised edition 1954. New York: De Capo Press.

Wilson, A. (1982). The national published record: Acquisition and preservation. *Bulletin of the John Rylands University Library of Manchester* 65, 246-264.

Wilson, P. (1983). *Second-hand knowledge: An enquiry into cognitive authority*. Westport, Conn.: Greenwood Press.

Wittgenstein, L. (1922). *Tractatus logico-philosophicus*. 1988. London: Routledge and Kegan Paul.

About the Author

Julian Warner is a faculty member in the School of Management and Economics, The Queen's University of Belfast.

He was a visiting scholar at the School of Library and Information Studies, University of California at Berkeley from 1991-1992 and at the Graduate School of Library and Information Science, University of Illinois in 2000.

His previous publications include *From Writing to Computers*. London and New York: Routledge, 1994.